MW01612768

THIS BOOK BELONGS TO

_____

_____

START DATE _____ / _____ / _____

HE READS TRUTH

FOUNDERS

FOUNDER
Raechel Myers

CO-FOUNDER
Amanda Bible Williams

EXECUTIVE

CHIEF EXECUTIVE OFFICER
Ryan Myers

CHIEF OPERATING OFFICER
Mark D. Bullard

EDITORIAL

MANAGING EDITOR
Lindsey Jacobi, MDiv

PRODUCTION EDITOR
Hannah Little, MTS

ASSOCIATE EDITOR
Kayla De La Torre, MAT

COPY EDITOR
Becca Owens, MA

CREATIVE

SENIOR ART DIRECTOR
Annie Glover

DESIGN MANAGER
Kelsea Allen

ART DIRECTOR
Lauren Haag

DESIGNER
Ashley Phillips

MARKETING

MARKETING DIRECTOR
Whitney Hoffmann

MARKETING PROJECT
COORDINATOR
Kyndal Kearns

GROWTH MARKETING MANAGERS
Katie Bevels
Blake Showalter

PRODUCT MARKETING MANAGER
Krista Squibb

CONTENT MARKETING STRATEGIST
Tameshia Williams, ThM

OPERATIONS

OPERATIONS DIRECTOR
Allison Sutton

OPERATIONS MANAGER
Mary Beth Steed

OPERATIONS ASSISTANT
Emily Andrews

SHIPPING

SHIPPING MANAGER
Marian Byne

FULFILLMENT LEAD
Kajsa Matheny

FULFILLMENT SPECIALISTS
Hannah Lamb
Kelsey Simpson

SUBSCRIPTION INQUIRIES
orders@hereadstruth.com

COMMUNITY SUPPORT

COMMUNITY SUPPORT MANAGER
Kara Hewett, MOL

COMMUNITY SUPPORT SPECIALISTS
Katy McKnight
Alecia Rohrer
Heather Vollono

CONTRIBUTORS

ART
Beth Winterburn

SPECIAL THANKS
Amy Dennis

COLOPHON

This book was printed offset in Nashville, Tennessee, on 60# Lynx Opaque Text under the direction of He Reads Truth. Cover is 100# Cougar Opaque with a soft touch lamination.

COPYRIGHT

© 2024 by He Reads Truth, LLC
All rights reserved.
All photography used by permission.

ISBN 978-1-962221-02-3

1 2 3 4 5 6 7 8 9 10

No part of this publication may be reproduced, distributed, or transmitted in any form or by any means, including photocopying, recording, or other electronic or mechanical methods, without the prior written permission of He Reads Truth, LLC, except in the case of brief quotations embodied in critical reviews and certain other noncommercial uses Unless ermitted by copyright law.

All Scripture is taken from the Christian Standard Bible®. Copyright © 2020 by Holman Bible Publishers. Used by permission. Christian Standard Bible® and CSB® are federally registered trademarks of Holman Bible Publishers.

Though the dates, locations, and names in this book have been carefully researched, scholars disagree on many of these topics.

Research support provided by Logos Bible Software™. Learn more at logos.com.

NUMBERS
THE LORD GOES WITH US

HE READS TRUTH

GOD'S CHARACTER IS
CONSTANT, AND HIS
PRESENCE PURSUES US.

I f we were to consider what a map of our lives might look like, it probably wouldn't appear as we expected. There are bound to be detours and dark places, unexpected joys and mountaintop moments. There's also an invisible thread that runs through it all—God's character is constant, and His presence pursues us.

The Old Testament book of Numbers is a kind of map. It is an account of Israel's indirect journey from Mount Sinai to the Jordan River, the forty years between their rescue from Egypt and their arrival at the border of the promised land. Their wilderness wandering—a consequence of their disobedience—is testimony of God's holiness. And it is a testimony of God's faithfulness, the setting in which God demonstrates His unwavering commitment to His people by pursuing them with His presence.

Numbers is a redemption story, but not just for the generation of Israelites who ate the manna and drank water from the rock. It is a redemption story for all nations and generations. Through the person and work of Jesus, we are all invited into the presence of the God whose holiness and compassion are like no other. Jesus Christ is the bread of life, the living water, the one whose perfect obedience redeems our wandering souls.

As you read Numbers, lean on the tools provided in this book. The "Numbers in Context" and "Types of Writing in Numbers" extras will give you a solid foundation for your study, and the map on page 158 will help you picture the Israelites' journey. Use the weekly response element to train your eyes to see the throughline of God and His character.

Wherever you stand on the timeline of your life, may God meet you here as we read His Word together. By the kindness and power of the Holy Spirit, may we come to understand more fully the beauty of obedience and the goodness of God's grace. The Lord goes with us! Thanks be to Him.

THE HE READS TRUTH TEAM

DESIGN ON PURPOSE

EACH HE READS TRUTH
RESOURCE IS THOUGHTFULLY
AND ARTFULLY DESIGNED
TO HIGHLIGHT THE BEAUTY,
GOODNESS, AND TRUTH OF
SCRIPTURE IN A WAY THAT
REFLECTS THE THEMES OF EACH
CURATED READING PLAN.

———

The *Numbers* Reading Guide features art from abstract artist, Beth Winterburn. Her work contains meandering brush strokes, looping circles, and lines of different shapes and sizes. These creative elements remind us of the bigger story being told of God and His people in the book of Numbers—as Israel wandered through the wilderness, God's faithfulness saw them through every twist and turn. Some of Beth's work is also reminiscent of the relief lines you find on old maps, and we've mirrored this theme in the grids and lines that pattern some of the pages.

The steady, timeless font points to the steadfast love that God had for His people, even in the middle of their wandering.

HOW TO USE THIS BOOK

He Reads Truth is a community of men dedicated to reading the Word of God every day. In this **Numbers** reading plan, we will read the book of Numbers, along with complimentary passages of Scripture, to reflect on God's continued faithfulness toward His people in the midst of their wandering and rebellion in the wilderness.

READ & REFLECT

Your **Numbers** book focuses primarily on Scripture, with added features to come alongside your time with God's Word.

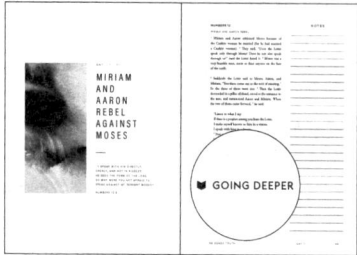

SCRIPTURE READING

Designed for a Monday start, this book presents the book of **Numbers** in daily readings, along with additional passages curated to show how the theme of the main reading can be found throughout Scripture.

Additional passages are marked in your daily reading with the Going Deeper heading.

REFLECTION QUESTIONS

Each week features questions and space for personal reflection.

COMMUNITY & CONVERSATION

You can start reading this book at any time. If you want to join men from across the globe as they read along with you, the He Reads Truth community will start Day 1 of **Numbers** on Monday, April 29, 2024.

GRACE DAY

Use Saturdays to catch up on your reading, pray, and rest in the presence of the Lord.

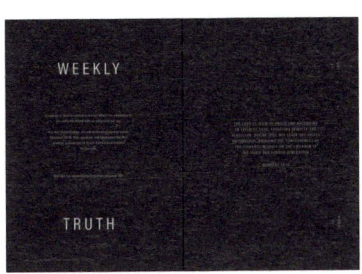

WEEKLY TRUTH

Sundays are set aside for Scripture memorization.

See tips for memorizing Scripture on page 180.

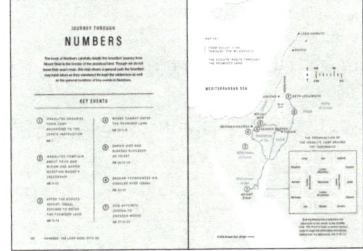

EXTRAS

This book features additional tools to help you gain a deeper understanding of the text.

Find a complete list of extras on pages 10-11.

HE READS TRUTH APP

Devotionals corresponding to each daily reading can be found in the **Numbers** reading plan on the He Reads Truth app. New devotionals will be published each weekday once the plan begins on Monday, April 29, 2024. You can use the app to participate in community discussion and more.

HEREADSTRUTH.COM

The **Numbers** reading plan and devotionals will also be available at HeReadsTruth.com as the community reads each day. Invite your family, friends, and neighbors to read along with you.

TABLE OF CONTENTS

THE LORD IS SLOW TO ANGER AND ABOUNDING
IN FAITHFUL LOVE, FORGIVING INIQUITY AND
REBELLION. BUT HE WILL NOT LEAVE THE GUILTY
UNPUNISHED, BRINGING THE CONSEQUENCES OF
THE FATHERS' INIQUITY ON THE CHILDREN TO THE
THIRD AND FOURTH GENERATION.

NUMBERS 14:18

INTRODUCTION
NUMBERS

ON THE TIMELINE

Like the rest of the Pentateuch, the writing of Numbers is traditionally attributed to Moses. Moses likely wrote this book before the nation of Israel entered Canaan, about 1406 BC. Numbers continues the historical narrative begun in Exodus, picking up one month after the close of Exodus (Ex 40:2; Nm 1:1), about one year after the Israelites' departure from Egypt in 1446 BC. Numbers covers the remaining thirty-nine years of the Israelites' stay in the wilderness, from Sinai to Kadesh, and finally to the plains on the eastern side of the Jordan River.

A LITTLE BACKGROUND

The English title "Numbers" derives from the name *Arithmoi*, used in the Greek translation of the Old Testament, based on the military censuses (chapters 1–4; 26). The Hebrew title, *Bemidbar*, which means "In the Wilderness," describes the geographical setting of much of the book—from the base of Mount Sinai to the wilderness to the arid plains of Moab, located east of the Dead Sea.

MESSAGE & PURPOSE

Because of their rebellion, the first generation of Israelites to come out of Egypt was not permitted to enter the promised land, the land God had promised to Abraham and his descendants.

Along with the other four books of the Pentateuch, Numbers provided reminders for Israel of God keeping His promises, of His bringing them through the wilderness, and the consequences of disobedience. The events recorded in Numbers demonstrated to the following generations of Israel that God is holy and pure and He requires those who claim Him as their God to reflect His holiness and purity.

GIVE THANKS FOR THE BOOK OF NUMBERS

The book of Numbers points us to God's continual invitation to faithfulness and His unwavering loyalty even when we fall short. By showing us how God responded to the unbelief of the Israelites, Numbers emphasizes the importance of obedience in the life of a Christian. Numbers demonstrates that there are consequences to our disobedience, while also reminding us that God's grace remains and His redemptive plan will not be stopped.

NUMBERS IN CONTEXT

The book of Numbers is the fourth book in the Pentateuch, the division of the Old Testament that encompasses the first five books of the Bible. The Pentateuch presents the origin of the earth, humankind, sin, and the institution of God's covenant. It is also where we discover the beginnings of the story of Israel, the nation set apart by God to bless the world.

Here is an overview of each book and a graphic below to help orient you to Israel's story in the context of the Pentateuch, from the creation of the first humans to Israel's preparation to enter into the promised land.

GENESIS

THE GARDEN OF EDEN

God created and blessed the world. He gave the first humans, Adam and Eve, a designated place to live in His presence and a mission to carry out His purpose for creation beyond Eden throughout the entire world. He promised life and abundance for following His instruction, but death as a result of disobedience. When Adam and Eve ultimately disobeyed, God again promised that a descendant of the woman would crush the serpent's head, signifying a coming end to sin and death. Scripture ultimately reveals that descendant as Jesus Christ.

THE PATRIARCHS

God called Abraham to leave his home in the land of Ur and follow Him to the land of Canaan. He made a covenant with Abraham, promising to make him the father of a great nation, give him Canaan as an inheritance, and bless the world through the offspring of his son Isaac. The descendants of Jacob's twelve sons became known as the twelve tribes of Israel, with each tribe bearing the name of one of Jacob's sons or grandsons.

Here is a graphic representation of the timespans of the events covered in each book of the Pentateuch and how they compare to one another.

GENESIS

EXODUS

THE EXODUS AND THE LAW

After the Israelites were enslaved in Egypt for nearly 400 years, God worked through Moses to rescue His people and lead them to freedom. At Mount Sinai, God made a covenant with the people of Israel, setting them apart as His chosen people in order to make His name known among all other nations. He also gave them the law, the standard by which they were to live in relationship with Him and worship Him alone.

LEVITICUS

THE TABERNACLE

As God established His covenant with the nation, He also instructed Moses to create the tabernacle (Ex 25–26), a sacred space for worship where God would dwell among His people. This mobile sanctuary, resembling a large tent, featured furnishings crafted with the finest materials and made to exact specifications to reflect God's holiness. In the book of Leviticus, God detailed the way in which imperfect people could come near His presence through a sacrificial system that addressed Israel's ever-present need for atonement because of the continual presence of sin. The people, through the mediation of the priests, came before God's presence with acceptable sacrifices and offerings.

NUMBERS

THE WILDERNESS WANDERINGS

When the Israelites scouted the land of Canaan that God had promised them, they were afraid and refused to enter. Because of their disobedience, God made the Israelites wander in the wilderness for forty years until the disobedient generation died.

DEUTERONOMY

THE PROMISED LAND

As the new generation of Israelites prepared to enter Canaan after forty years of wandering in the wilderness, Moses repeated the law that God established at Sinai. God renewed His promise to bless them with land if they obeyed His statutes. He also detailed the consequences they would encounter if they chose to rebel against Him. God used the nation of Israel to begin the work of redeeming the land and everything in it, fulfilling His promise that Abraham's descendants would settle in the land God would give them.

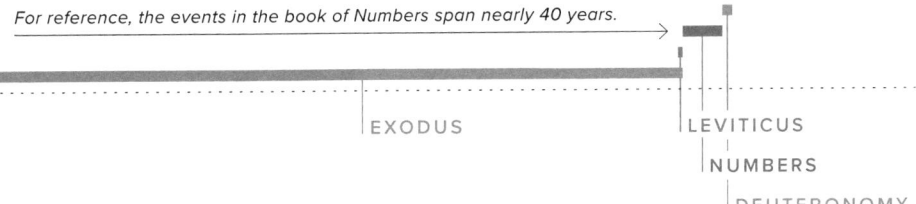

For reference, the events in the book of Numbers span nearly 40 years.

EXODUS

LEVITICUS

NUMBERS

DEUTERONOMY

© 2024 He Reads Truth. All rights reserved.

ORGANIZATION OF THE CAMP

NUMBERS 1

THE CENSUS OF ISRAEL

[1] The LORD spoke to Moses in the tent of meeting in the Wilderness of Sinai, on the first day of the second month of the second year after Israel's departure from the land of Egypt: [2] "Take a census of the entire Israelite community by their clans and their ancestral families, counting the names of every male one by one. [3] You and Aaron are to register those who are twenty years old or more by their military divisions—everyone who can serve in Israel's army. [4] A man from each tribe is to be with you, each one the head of his ancestral family. [5] These are the names of the men who are to assist you:

Elizur son of Shedeur from Reuben;
[6] Shelumiel son of Zurishaddai from Simeon;
[7] Nahshon son of Amminadab from Judah;
[8] Nethanel son of Zuar from Issachar;
[9] Eliab son of Helon from Zebulun;
[10] from the sons of Joseph:
Elishama son of Ammihud from Ephraim,
Gamaliel son of Pedahzur from Manasseh;
[11] Abidan son of Gideoni from Benjamin;
[12] Ahiezer son of Ammishaddai from Dan;
[13] Pagiel son of Ochran from Asher;
[14] Eliasaph son of Deuel from Gad;
[15] Ahira son of Enan from Naphtali.

[16] These are the men called from the community; they are leaders of their ancestral tribes, the heads of Israel's clans."

[17] So Moses and Aaron took these men who had been designated by name, [18] and they assembled the whole community on the first day of the second month. They recorded their ancestry by their clans and their ancestral families,

counting one by one the names of those twenty years old or more, [19] just as the LORD commanded Moses. He registered them in the Wilderness of Sinai:

[20] The descendants of Reuben, the firstborn of Israel: according to their family records by their clans and their ancestral families, counting one by one the names of every male twenty years old or more, everyone who could serve in the army, [21] those registered for the tribe of Reuben numbered 46,500.

[22] The descendants of Simeon: according to their family records by their clans and their ancestral families, those registered counting one by one the names of every male twenty years old or more, everyone who could serve in the army, [23] those registered for the tribe of Simeon numbered 59,300.

[24] The descendants of Gad: according to their family records by their clans and their ancestral families, counting the names of those twenty years old or more, everyone who could serve in the army, [25] those registered for the tribe of Gad numbered 45,650.

[26] The descendants of Judah: according to their family records by their clans and their ancestral families, counting the names of those twenty years old or more, everyone who could serve in the army, [27] those registered for the tribe of Judah numbered 74,600.

[28] The descendants of Issachar: according to their family records by their clans and their ancestral families, counting the names of those twenty years old or more, everyone who could serve in the army, [29] those registered for the tribe of Issachar numbered 54,400.

[30] The descendants of Zebulun: according to their family records by their clans and their ancestral families, counting the names of those twenty years

Throughout this reading plan you will find margin notes that provide helpful context to the day's reading or show how Numbers connects to other places in Scripture.

THE COMMUNAL IDENTITY OF ISRAEL

In the book of Numbers, there is a close relationship between the communal identity of the nation of Israel and the daily lives of God's people. God communicated His will through the commands He gave to the whole nation, and the individual actions of members of the community were shaped by those shared values.

old or more, everyone who could serve in the army, [31] those registered for the tribe of Zebulun numbered 57,400.

[32] The descendants of Joseph:

The descendants of Ephraim: according to their family records by their clans and their ancestral families, counting the names of those twenty years old or more, everyone who could serve in the army, [33] those registered for the tribe of Ephraim numbered 40,500.

[34] The descendants of Manasseh: according to their family records by their clans and their ancestral families, counting the names of those twenty years old or more, everyone who could serve in the army, [35] those registered for the tribe of Manasseh numbered 32,200.

[36] The descendants of Benjamin: according to their family records by their clans and their ancestral families, counting the names of those twenty years old or more, everyone who could serve in the army, [37] those registered for the tribe of Benjamin numbered 35,400.

[38] The descendants of Dan: according to their family records by their clans and their ancestral families, counting the names of those twenty years old or more, everyone who could serve in the army, [39] those registered for the tribe of Dan numbered 62,700.

[40] The descendants of Asher: according to their family records by their clans and their ancestral families, counting the names of those twenty years old or more, everyone who could serve in the army, [41] those registered for the tribe of Asher numbered 41,500.

[42] The descendants of Naphtali: according to their family records by their clans and their ancestral families, counting the names of those twenty years old or more, everyone who could serve in the army, [43] those registered for the tribe of Naphtali numbered 53,400.

[44] These are the men Moses and Aaron registered, with the assistance of the twelve leaders of Israel; each represented his ancestral family. [45] So all the Israelites twenty years old or more, everyone who could serve in Israel's army, were registered by their ancestral families. [46] All those registered numbered 603,550.

DUTIES OF THE LEVITES

[47] But the Levites were not registered with them by their ancestral tribe. [48] For the Lord had told Moses, [49] "Do not register or take a census of the tribe of Levi with the other Israelites.

[50] APPOINT THE LEVITES OVER THE TABERNACLE OF THE TESTIMONY,

all its furnishings, and everything in it. They are to transport the tabernacle and all its articles, take care of it, and camp around it. [51] Whenever the tabernacle is to move, the Levites are to take it down, and whenever it is to stop at a campsite, the Levites are to set it up. Any unauthorized person who comes near it is to be put to death.

[52] "The Israelites are to camp by their military divisions, each man with his encampment and under his banner. [53] The Levites are to camp around the tabernacle of the testimony and watch over it, so that no wrath will fall on the

Israelite community." [54] The Israelites did everything just as the LORD had commanded Moses.

NUMBERS 2

ORGANIZATION OF THE CAMPS

[1] The LORD spoke to Moses and Aaron: [2] "The Israelites are to camp under their respective banners beside the flags of their ancestral families. They are to camp around the tent of meeting at a distance from it:

[3] Judah's military divisions will camp on the east side toward the sunrise under their banner. The leader of the descendants of Judah is Nahshon son of Amminadab. [4] His military division numbers 74,600. [5] The tribe of Issachar will camp next to it. The leader of the Issacharites is Nethanel son of Zuar. [6] His military division numbers 54,400. [7] The tribe of Zebulun will be next. The leader of the Zebulunites is Eliab son of Helon. [8] His military division numbers 57,400. [9] The total number in their military divisions who belong to Judah's encampment is 186,400; they will move out first.

[10] Reuben's military divisions will camp on the south side under their banner. The leader of the Reubenites is Elizur son of Shedeur. [11] His military division numbers 46,500. [12] The tribe of Simeon will camp next to it. The leader of the Simeonites is Shelumiel son of Zurishaddai. [13] His military division numbers 59,300. [14] The tribe of Gad will be next. The leader of the Gadites is Eliasaph son of Deuel. [15] His military division numbers 45,650. [16] The total number in their military divisions who belong to Reuben's encampment is 151,450; they will move out second.

[17] The tent of meeting is to move out with the Levites' camp, which is in the middle of the camps.

They are to move out just as they camp, each in his place, with their banners.

18 Ephraim's military divisions will camp on the west side under their banner. The leader of the Ephraimites is Elishama son of Ammihud. 19 His military division numbers 40,500. 20 The tribe of Manasseh will be next to it. The leader of the Manassites is Gamaliel son of Pedahzur. 21 His military division numbers 32,200. 22 The tribe of Benjamin will be next. The leader of the Benjaminites is Abidan son of Gideoni. 23 His military division numbers 35,400. 24 The total in their military divisions who belong to Ephraim's encampment number 108,100; they will move out third.

25 Dan's military divisions will camp on the north side under their banner. The leader of the Danites is Ahiezer son of Ammishaddai. 26 His military division numbers 62,700. 27 The tribe of Asher will camp next to it. The leader of the Asherites is Pagiel son of Ochran. 28 His military division numbers 41,500. 29 The tribe of Naphtali will be next. The leader of the Naphtalites is Ahira son of Enan. 30 His military division numbers 53,400. 31 The total number who belong to Dan's encampment is 157,600; they are to move out last, with their banners."

32 These are the Israelites registered by their ancestral families. The total number in the camps by their military divisions is 603,550. 33 But the Levites were not registered among the Israelites, just as the LORD had commanded Moses.

34 The Israelites did everything the LORD commanded Moses; they camped by their banners in this way and moved out the same way, each man by his clan and by his ancestral family.

♥ GOING DEEPER

EXODUS 29:45-46

45 "I will dwell among the Israelites and be their God. 46 And they will know that I am the LORD their God, who brought them out of the land of Egypt, so that I might dwell among them. I am the LORD their God."

REVELATION 21:9-22

THE NEW JERUSALEM

9 Then one of the seven angels, who had held the seven bowls filled with the seven last plagues, came and spoke with me: "Come, I will show you the bride, the wife of the Lamb." 10 He then carried me away in the Spirit to a great, high mountain and showed me the holy city, Jerusalem, coming down out of heaven from God, 11 arrayed with God's glory. Her radiance was like a precious jewel, like a jasper stone, clear as crystal. 12 The city had a massive high wall, with twelve gates. Twelve angels were at the gates; the names of the twelve tribes of Israel's sons were inscribed on the gates. 13 There were three gates on the east, three gates on the north, three gates on the south, and three gates on the west. 14 The city wall had twelve foundations, and the twelve names of the twelve apostles of the Lamb were on the foundations.

15 The one who spoke with me had a golden measuring rod to measure the city, its gates, and its wall. 16 The city is laid out in a square; its length and width are the same. He measured the city with the rod at 12,000 *stadia*. Its length, width, and height are equal. 17 Then he measured its wall, 144 cubits according to

human measurement, which the angel used. [18] The building material of its wall was jasper, and the city was pure gold clear as glass. [19] The foundations of the city wall were adorned with every kind of jewel: the first foundation is jasper, the second sapphire, the third chalcedony, the fourth emerald, [20] the fifth sardonyx, the sixth carnelian, the seventh chrysolite, the eighth beryl, the ninth topaz, the tenth chrysoprase, the eleventh jacinth, the twelfth amethyst. [21] The twelve gates are twelve pearls; each individual gate was made of a single pearl. The main street of the city was pure gold, transparent as glass.

[22] I did not see a temple in it, because the Lord God the Almighty and the Lamb are its temple.

02

DAY

AARON'S SONS
AND THE LEVITES

NUMBERS 3

AARON'S SONS AND THE LEVITES

[1] These are the family records of Aaron and Moses at the time the LORD spoke with Moses on Mount Sinai. [2] These are the names of Aaron's sons: Nadab, the firstborn, and Abihu, Eleazar, and Ithamar. [3] These are the names of Aaron's sons, the anointed priests, who were ordained to serve as priests. [4] But Nadab and Abihu died in the LORD's presence when they presented unauthorized fire before the LORD in the Wilderness of Sinai, and they had no sons. So Eleazar and Ithamar served as priests under the direction of Aaron their father.

[5] The LORD spoke to Moses: [6] "Bring the tribe of Levi near and present them to the priest Aaron to assist him. [7] They are to perform duties for him and the entire community before the tent of meeting by attending to the service of the tabernacle. [8] They are to take care of all the furnishings of the tent of meeting and perform duties for the Israelites by attending to the service of the tabernacle.

[9] ASSIGN THE LEVITES TO AARON AND HIS SONS; THEY HAVE BEEN ASSIGNED EXCLUSIVELY TO HIM FROM THE ISRAELITES.

[10] You are to appoint Aaron and his sons to carry out their priestly responsibilities, but any unauthorized person who comes near the sanctuary is to be put to death."

[11] The LORD spoke to Moses: [12] "See, I have taken the Levites from the Israelites in place of every firstborn Israelite from the womb. The Levites belong to me, [13] because every firstborn belongs to me. At the time I struck down every firstborn in the land of Egypt, I consecrated every firstborn in Israel to myself, both man and animal. They are mine; I am the LORD."

THE LEVITICAL CENSUS

[14] The LORD spoke to Moses in the Wilderness of Sinai: [15] "Register the Levites by their ancestral families and their clans. You are to register every male one month old or more."

16 So Moses registered them in obedience to the LORD as he had been commanded:

17 These were Levi's sons by name: Gershon, Kohath, and Merari. 18 These were the names of Gershon's sons by their clans: Libni and Shimei. 19 Kohath's sons by their clans were Amram, Izhar, Hebron, and Uzziel. 20 Merari's sons by their clans were Mahli and Mushi. These were the Levite clans by their ancestral families.

21 The Libnite clan and the Shimeite clan came from Gershon; these were the Gershonite clans. 22 Those registered, counting every male one month old or more, numbered 7,500. 23 The Gershonite clans camped behind the tabernacle on the west side, 24 and the leader of the Gershonite families was Eliasaph son of Lael. 25 The Gershonites' duties at the tent of meeting involved the tabernacle, the tent, its covering, the screen for the entrance to the tent of meeting, 26 the hangings of the courtyard, the screen for the entrance to the courtyard that surrounds the tabernacle and the altar, and the tent ropes—all the work relating to these.

27 The Amramite clan, the Izharite clan, the Hebronite clan, and the Uzzielite clan came from Kohath; these were the Kohathites. 28 Counting every male one month old or more, there were 8,600 responsible for the duties of the sanctuary. 29 The clans of the Kohathites camped on the south side of the tabernacle, 30 and the leader of the families of the Kohathite clans was Elizaphan son of Uzziel. 31 Their duties involved the ark, the table, the lampstand, the altars, the sanctuary utensils that were used with these, and the screen—and all the work relating to them. 32 The chief of the Levite leaders was Eleazar son of Aaron the priest; he had oversight of those responsible for the duties of the sanctuary.

33 The Mahlite clan and the Mushite clan came from Merari; these were the Merarite clans. 34 Those registered, counting every male one month old or more, numbered 6,200. 35 The leader of the families of the Merarite clans was Zuriel son of Abihail; they camped on the north side of the tabernacle. 36 The assigned duties of Merari's descendants involved the tabernacle's supports, crossbars, pillars, bases, all its equipment, and all the work related to these, 37 in addition to the posts of the surrounding courtyard with their bases, tent pegs, and ropes.

38 Moses, Aaron, and his sons, who performed the duties of the sanctuary as a service on behalf of the Israelites, camped in front of the tabernacle on the east, in front of the tent of meeting toward the sunrise. Any unauthorized person who came near it was to be put to death.

39 The total number of all the Levite males one month old or more that Moses and Aaron registered by their clans at the LORD's command was 22,000.

"BRING THE TRIBE OF LEVI NEAR AND PRESENT THEM TO THE PRIEST AARON TO ASSIST HIM."

NUMBERS 3:6

40 The LORD told Moses, "Register every firstborn male of the Israelites one month old or more, and list their names. 41 You are to take the Levites for me—I am the LORD—in place of every firstborn among the Israelites, and the Levites' cattle in place of every firstborn among the Israelites' cattle." 42 So Moses registered every firstborn among the Israelites, as the LORD commanded him. 43 The total number of the firstborn males one month old or more listed by name was 22,273.

44 The LORD spoke to Moses again: 45 "Take the Levites in place of every firstborn among the Israelites, and the Levites' cattle in place of their cattle. The Levites belong to me; I am the LORD. 46 As the redemption price for the 273 firstborn Israelites who outnumber the Levites, 47 collect five shekels for each person, according to the standard sanctuary shekel—twenty gerahs to the shekel. 48 Give the silver to Aaron and his sons as the redemption price for those who are in excess among the Israelites."

49 So Moses collected the redemption amount from those in excess of the ones redeemed by the Levites. 50 He collected the silver from the firstborn Israelites: 1,365 shekels measured by the standard sanctuary shekel. 51 He gave the redemption silver to Aaron and his sons in obedience to the LORD, just as the LORD commanded Moses.

NUMBERS 4

DUTIES OF THE KOHATHITES

1 The LORD spoke to Moses and Aaron: 2 "Among the Levites, take a census of the Kohathites by their clans and their ancestral families, 3 men from thirty years old to fifty years old—everyone who is qualified to do work at the tent of meeting.

4 "The service of the Kohathites at the tent of meeting concerns the most holy objects. 5 Whenever the camp is about to move on, Aaron and his sons are to go in, take down the screening curtain, and cover the ark of the testimony with it. 6 They are to place over this a covering made of fine leather, spread a solid blue cloth on top, and insert its poles.

7 "They are to spread a blue cloth over the table of the Presence and place the plates and cups on it, as well as the bowls and pitchers for the drink offering. The regular bread offering is to be on it. 8 They are to spread a scarlet cloth over them, cover them with a covering made of fine leather, and insert the poles in the table.

9 "They are to take a blue cloth and cover the lampstand used for light, with its lamps, snuffers, and firepans, as well as its jars of oil by which they service it. 10 Then they are to place it with all its utensils inside a covering made of fine leather and put them on the carrying frame.

11 "They are to spread a blue cloth over the gold altar, cover it with a covering made of fine leather, and insert its poles. 12 They are to take all the serving utensils they use in the sanctuary, place them in a blue cloth, cover them with a covering made of fine leather, and put them on a carrying frame.

13 "They are to remove the ashes from the bronze altar, spread a purple cloth over it, 14 and place all the equipment on it that they use in serving: the firepans, meat forks, shovels, and basins—all the equipment of the altar.

They are to spread a covering made of fine leather over it and insert its poles.

15 "Aaron and his sons are to finish covering the holy objects and all their equipment whenever the camp is to move on. The Kohathites will come and carry them, but they are not to touch the holy objects or they will die. These are the transportation duties of the Kohathites regarding the tent of meeting.

16 "Eleazar, son of Aaron the priest, has oversight of the lamp oil, the fragrant incense, the daily grain offering, and the anointing oil. He has oversight of the entire tabernacle and everything in it, the holy objects and their utensils."

17 Then the LORD spoke to Moses and Aaron: 18 "Do not allow the Kohathite tribal clans to be wiped out from the Levites. 19 Do this for them so that they may live and not die when they come near the most holy objects: Aaron and his sons are to go in and assign each man his task and transportation duty. 20 The Kohathites are not to go in and look at the holy objects as they are covered or they will die."

DUTIES OF THE GERSHONITES

21 The LORD spoke to Moses: 22 "Take a census of the Gershonites also, by their ancestral families and their clans. 23 Register men from thirty years old to fifty years old, everyone who is qualified to perform service, to do work at the tent of meeting. 24 This is the service of the Gershonite clans regarding work and transportation duties: 25 They are to transport the tabernacle curtains, the tent of meeting with its covering and the covering made of fine leather on top of it, the screen for the entrance to the tent of meeting, 26 the hangings of the courtyard, the screen for the entrance at the gate of the courtyard that surrounds the tabernacle and the altar, along with their ropes and all the equipment for their service.

NOTES

They will carry out everything that needs to be done with these items.

27 "All the service of the Gershonites, all their transportation duties and all their other work, is to be done at the command of Aaron and his sons; you are to assign to them all that they are responsible to carry. 28 This is the service of the Gershonite clans at the tent of meeting, and their duties will be under the direction of Ithamar son of Aaron the priest.

DUTIES OF THE MERARITES

29 "As for the Merarites, you are to register them by their clans and their ancestral families. 30 Register men from thirty years old to fifty years old, everyone who is qualified to do the work of the tent of meeting. 31 This is what they are responsible to carry as the whole of their service at the tent of meeting: the supports of the tabernacle, with its crossbars, pillars, and bases, 32 the posts of the surrounding courtyard with their bases, tent pegs, and ropes, including all their equipment and all the work related to them. You are to assign by name the items that they are responsible to carry. 33 This is the service of the Merarite clans regarding all their work at the tent of meeting, under the direction of Ithamar son of Aaron the priest."

CENSUS OF THE LEVITES

34 So Moses, Aaron, and the leaders of the community registered the Kohathites by their clans and their ancestral families, 35 men from thirty years old to fifty years old, everyone who was qualified for work at the tent of meeting. 36 The men registered by their clans numbered 2,750. 37 These were the registered men of the Kohathite clans, everyone who could serve at the tent of meeting. Moses and Aaron registered them at the LORD's command through Moses.

38 The Gershonites were registered by their clans and their ancestral families, 39 men from thirty years old to fifty years old, everyone who was qualified for work at the tent of meeting. 40 The men registered by their clans and their ancestral families numbered 2,630. 41 These were the registered men of the Gershonite clans. At the LORD's command Moses and Aaron registered everyone who could serve at the tent of meeting.

42 The men of the Merarite clans were registered by their clans and their ancestral families, 43 those from thirty years old to fifty years old, everyone who was qualified for work at the tent of meeting. 44 The men registered by their clans numbered 3,200. 45 These were the registered men of the Merarite clans; Moses and Aaron registered them at the LORD's command through Moses.

46 Moses, Aaron, and the leaders of Israel registered all the Levites by their clans and their ancestral families, 47 from thirty years old to fifty years old, everyone who was qualified to do the work of serving at the tent of meeting and transporting it. 48 Their registered men numbered 8,580. 49 At the LORD's command they were registered under the direction of Moses, each one according to his work and transportation duty, and his assignment was as the LORD commanded Moses.

🔖 GOING DEEPER

DEUTERONOMY 18:1-5

PROVISIONS FOR THE LEVITES

1 The Levitical priests, the whole tribe of Levi, will have no portion or inheritance with Israel. They will eat the LORD's food offerings; that is their inheritance. 2 Although Levi has

no inheritance among his brothers, the LORD is his inheritance, as he promised him. [3] This is the priests' share from the people who offer a sacrifice, whether it is an ox, a sheep, or a goat; the priests are to be given the shoulder, jaws, and stomach. [4] You are to give him the firstfruits of your grain, new wine, and fresh oil, and the first sheared wool of your flock.

[5] FOR THE LORD YOUR GOD HAS CHOSEN HIM AND HIS SONS FROM ALL YOUR TRIBES TO STAND AND MINISTER IN HIS NAME FROM NOW ON.

HEBREWS 7:23-28

[23] Now many have become Levitical priests, since they are prevented by death from remaining in office. [24] But because he remains forever, he holds his priesthood permanently. [25] Therefore, he is able to save completely those who come to God through him, since he always lives to intercede for them.

[26] For this is the kind of high priest we need: holy, innocent, undefiled, separated from sinners, and exalted above the heavens. [27] He doesn't need to offer sacrifices every day, as high priests do—first for their own sins, then for those of the people. He did this once for all time when he offered himself. [28] For the law appoints as high priests men who are weak, but the promise of the oath, which came after the law, appoints a Son, who has been perfected forever.

COMPENSATION

FOR

WRONGDOING

NUMBERS 5

ISOLATION OF THE UNCLEAN

[1] The LORD instructed Moses, [2] "Command the Israelites to send away anyone from the camp who is afflicted with a skin disease, anyone who has a discharge, or anyone who is defiled because of a corpse. [3] Send away both male or female; send them outside the camp, so that they will not defile their camps where I dwell among them." [4] The Israelites did this, sending them outside the camp. The Israelites did as the LORD instructed Moses.

COMPENSATION FOR WRONGDOING

[5] The LORD spoke to Moses: [6] "Tell the Israelites: When a man or woman commits any sin against another, that person acts unfaithfully toward the LORD and is guilty. [7] The person is to confess the sin he has committed. He is to pay full compensation, add a fifth of its value to it, and give it to the individual he has wronged. [8] But if that individual has no relative to receive compensation, the compensation goes to the LORD for the priest, along with the atonement ram by which the priest will make atonement for the guilty person. [9] Every holy contribution the Israelites present to the priest will be his. [10] Each one's holy contribution is his to give; what each one gives to the priest will be his."

THE JEALOUSY RITUAL

[11] The LORD spoke to Moses: [12] "Speak to the Israelites and tell them: If any man's wife goes astray, is unfaithful to him, [13] and sleeps with another, but it is concealed from her husband, and she is undetected, even though she has defiled herself, since there is no witness against her, and she wasn't caught in the act; [14] and if a feeling of jealousy comes over the husband and he becomes jealous because of his wife who has defiled herself—or if a feeling of jealousy comes over him and he becomes jealous of her though she has not defiled herself— [15] then the man is to bring his wife to the priest. He is also to bring an offering for her of two quarts of barley flour. He is not to pour oil over it or put frankincense on it because it is a grain offering of jealousy, a grain offering for remembrance to draw attention to guilt.

[16] "The priest is to bring her forward and have her stand before the LORD. [17] Then the priest is to take holy water in a clay bowl, take some of the dust from the tabernacle floor, and put it in the water. [18] After the priest has the woman stand before the LORD, he is to let down her hair and place in her hands the grain offering for remembrance, which is the grain offering of jealousy. The priest is to hold the bitter water that brings a curse. [19] The priest will require the woman to take an oath and will say to her, 'If no man has slept with you, if you have not gone astray and become defiled while under your husband's authority, be unaffected by this bitter water that brings a curse. [20] But if you have gone astray while under your husband's authority, if you have defiled yourself and a man other than your husband has slept with you'— [21] at this point the priest will make the woman take the oath with the sworn curse, and he is to say to her—'May the LORD make you into an object of your people's cursing and swearing when he makes your womb shrivel and your belly swell. [22] May this water that brings a curse enter your stomach, causing your belly to swell and your womb to shrivel.'

"And the woman will reply, 'Amen, Amen.'

23 "Then the priest is to write these curses on a scroll and wash them off into the bitter water. 24 He will require the woman to drink the bitter water that brings a curse, and it will enter her to cause bitter suffering. 25 The priest is to take the grain offering of jealousy from the woman, present the offering before the LORD, and bring it to the altar. 26 The priest is to take a handful of the grain offering as a memorial portion and burn it on the altar. Afterward, he will require the woman to drink the water.

27 "When he makes her drink the water, if she has defiled herself and been unfaithful to her husband, the water that brings a curse will enter her to cause bitter suffering; her belly will swell, and her womb will shrivel. She will become a curse among her people. 28 But if the woman has not defiled herself and is pure, she will be unaffected and will be able to conceive children.

29 "This is the law regarding jealousy when a wife goes astray and defiles herself while under her husband's authority, 30 or when a feeling of jealousy comes over a husband and he becomes jealous of his wife. He is to have the woman stand before the LORD, and the priest will carry out all these instructions for her. 31 The husband will be free of guilt, but that woman will bear her iniquity."

❤ GOING DEEPER

LEVITICUS 5:17–19

17 "If someone sins and without knowing it violates any of the LORD's commands concerning anything prohibited, he is guilty, and he will bear his iniquity. 18 He must bring an unblemished ram from the

flock according to your assessment of its value as a guilt offering to the priest. Then the priest will make atonement on his behalf for the error he has committed unintentionally, and he will be forgiven. [19] It is a guilt offering; he is indeed guilty before the LORD."

LEVITICUS 6:1-7

[1] The LORD spoke to Moses: [2] "When someone sins and offends the LORD by deceiving his neighbor in regard to a deposit, a security, or a robbery; or defrauds his neighbor; [3] or finds something lost and lies about it; or swears falsely about any of the sinful things a person may do— [4] once he has sinned and acknowledged his guilt—he must return what he stole or defrauded, or the deposit entrusted to him, or the lost item he found, [5] or anything else about which he swore falsely. He will make full restitution for it and add a fifth of its value to it. He is to pay it to its owner on the day he acknowledges his guilt. [6] Then he is to bring his guilt offering to the LORD: an unblemished ram from the flock according to your assessment of its value as a guilt offering to the priest. [7] In this way the priest will make atonement on his behalf before the LORD, and he will be forgiven for anything he may have done to incur guilt."

1 JOHN 1:9

IF WE CONFESS OUR SINS, HE IS FAITHFUL AND RIGHTEOUS TO FORGIVE US OUR SINS AND TO CLEANSE US FROM ALL UNRIGHTEOUSNESS.

THE

DAY

NAZIRITE

04

VOW

THE NAZIRITE VOW

[1] The LORD instructed Moses, [2] "Speak to the Israelites and tell them: When a man or woman makes a special vow, a Nazirite vow, to consecrate himself to the LORD, [3] he is to abstain from wine and beer. He must not drink vinegar made from wine or from beer. He must not drink any grape juice or eat fresh grapes or raisins. [4] He is not to eat anything produced by the grapevine, from seeds to skin, during the period of his consecration.

[5] "You must not cut his hair throughout the time of his vow of consecration. He may be holy until the time is completed during which he consecrates himself to the LORD; he is to let the hair of his head grow long. [6] He must not go near a dead body during the time he consecrates himself to the LORD. [7] He is not to defile himself for his father or mother, or his brother or sister, when they die, while the mark of consecration to his God is on his head. [8] He is holy to the LORD during the time of consecration.

[9] "If someone suddenly dies near him, defiling his consecrated head, he must shave his head on the day of his purification; he is to shave it on the seventh day. [10] On the eighth day he is to bring two turtledoves or two young pigeons to the priest at the entrance to the tent of meeting. [11] The priest is to offer one as a sin offering and the other as a burnt offering to make atonement on behalf of the Nazirite, since he incurred guilt because of the corpse. On that day he is to consecrate his head again. [12] He is to rededicate his time of consecration to the LORD and to bring a year-old male lamb as a guilt offering. But do not count the initial period of consecration because it became defiled.

[13] "This is the law of the Nazirite: On the day his time of consecration is completed, he is to be brought to the entrance to the tent of meeting. [14] He is to present an offering to the LORD of one unblemished year-old male lamb as a burnt offering, one unblemished year-old female lamb as a sin offering, one unblemished ram as a fellowship offering, [15] along with their grain offerings and drink offerings, and a basket of unleavened cakes made from fine flour mixed with oil, and unleavened wafers coated with oil.

[16] "The priest is to present these before the LORD and sacrifice the Nazirite's sin offering and burnt offering. [17] He will also offer the ram as a fellowship sacrifice to the LORD, together with the basket of unleavened bread. Then the priest will offer the accompanying grain offering and drink offering.

[18] "The Nazirite is to shave his consecrated head at the entrance to the tent of meeting, take the hair from his head, and put it on the fire under the fellowship sacrifice. [19] The priest is to take the boiled shoulder from the ram, one unleavened cake from the basket, and one unleavened wafer, and put them into the hands of the Nazirite after he has shaved his consecrated head. [20] The priest is to present them as a presentation offering before the LORD. It is a holy portion for the priest, in addition to the breast of the presentation offering and the thigh of the contribution. After that, the Nazirite may drink wine.

21 "These are the instructions about the Nazirite who vows his offering to the LORD for his consecration, in addition to whatever else he can afford; he must fulfill whatever vow he makes in keeping with the instructions for his consecration."

THE PRIESTLY BLESSING

22 The LORD spoke to Moses: 23 "Tell Aaron and his sons, 'This is how you are to bless the Israelites. You should say to them,

24 "May the LORD bless you and protect you;
25 may the LORD make his face shine on you and be gracious to you;
26 may the LORD look with favor on you and give you peace."'

27 In this way they will pronounce my name over the Israelites, and I will bless them."

🔖 GOING DEEPER

LUKE 1:5-17

GABRIEL PREDICTS JOHN'S BIRTH

5 In the days of King Herod of Judea, there was a priest of Abijah's division named Zechariah. His wife was from the daughters of Aaron, and her name was Elizabeth. 6 Both were righteous in God's sight, living without blame according to all the commands and requirements of the Lord. 7 But they had no children because Elizabeth could not conceive, and both of them were well along in years.

8 When his division was on duty and he was serving as priest before God, 9 it happened that he was chosen by lot, according to the custom of the priesthood, to enter the sanctuary of the Lord and burn incense. 10 At the hour of incense the whole assembly of the people was praying outside. 11 An angel of the Lord appeared to him, standing to the right of the altar of incense. 12 When Zechariah saw him, he was terrified and overcome with fear. 13 But the angel said to him, "Do not be afraid, Zechariah, because your prayer has been heard. Your wife Elizabeth will bear you a son, and you will name him John. 14 There will be joy and delight for you, and many will rejoice at his birth. 15 For he will be great in the sight of the Lord and will never drink wine or beer. He will be filled with the Holy Spirit while still in his mother's womb. 16 He will turn many of the children of Israel to the Lord their God. 17 And he will go before him in the spirit and power of Elijah, to turn the hearts of fathers to their children, and the disobedient to the understanding of the righteous, to make ready for the Lord a prepared people."

2 TIMOTHY 2:21-22

21 So if anyone purifies himself from anything dishonorable, he will be a special instrument, set apart, useful to the Master, prepared for every good work.

22 Flee from youthful passions, and pursue righteousness, faith, love, and peace, along with those who call on the Lord from a pure heart.

NOTES

OFFERINGS FROM THE LEADERS

———

THE LEADERS OF ISRAEL,
THE HEADS OF THEIR
ANCESTRAL FAMILIES,
PRESENTED AN OFFERING.

NUMBERS 7:2

OFFERINGS FROM THE LEADERS

¹ On the day Moses finished setting up the tabernacle, he anointed and consecrated it and all its furnishings, along with the altar and all its utensils. After he anointed and consecrated these things, ² the leaders of Israel, the heads of their ancestral families, presented an offering. They were the tribal leaders who supervised the registration. ³ They brought as their offering before the LORD six covered carts and twelve oxen, a cart from every two leaders and an ox from each one, and presented them in front of the tabernacle.

⁴ The LORD said to Moses, ⁵ "Accept these from them to be used in the work of the tent of meeting, and give this offering to the Levites, to each division according to their service."

⁶ So Moses took the carts and oxen and gave them to the Levites. ⁷ He gave the Gershonites two carts and four oxen corresponding to their service, ⁸ and gave the Merarites four carts and eight oxen corresponding to their service, under the direction of Ithamar son of Aaron the priest. ⁹ But he did not give any to the Kohathites, since their responsibility was service related to the holy objects carried on their shoulders.

¹⁰ THE LEADERS ALSO PRESENTED THE DEDICATION GIFT FOR THE ALTAR WHEN IT WAS ANOINTED.

The leaders presented their offerings in front of the altar. ¹¹ The LORD told Moses, "Each day have one leader present his offering for the dedication of the altar."

¹² The one who presented his offering on the first day was Nahshon son of Amminadab from the tribe of Judah. ¹³ His offering was one silver dish weighing 3¼ pounds and one silver basin weighing 1¾ pounds, measured by the standard sanctuary shekel, both of them full of fine flour mixed with oil for a grain offering; ¹⁴ one gold bowl weighing four ounces, full of incense; ¹⁵ one young bull, one ram, and one male lamb a year old, for a burnt offering; ¹⁶ one male goat for a sin offering; ¹⁷ and two bulls, five rams, five male goats, and five male lambs a year old, for the fellowship sacrifice. This was the offering of Nahshon son of Amminadab.

¹⁸ On the second day Nethanel son of Zuar, leader of Issachar, presented an offering. ¹⁹ As his offering, he presented one silver dish weighing 3¼ pounds and one silver basin weighing 1¾ pounds, measured by the standard sanctuary shekel, both of them full of fine flour mixed with oil for a grain offering; ²⁰ one gold bowl weighing four ounces, full of incense; ²¹ one young bull, one ram, and one male lamb a year old, for a burnt offering; ²² one male goat for a sin offering; ²³ and two bulls, five rams, five male goats, and five male lambs a year old, for the fellowship sacrifice. This was the offering of Nethanel son of Zuar.

²⁴ On the third day Eliab son of Helon, leader of the Zebulunites, presented an offering. ²⁵ His offering was one silver dish weighing 3¼ pounds and one silver basin weighing 1¾ pounds, measured by the standard sanctuary shekel, both of them full of fine flour mixed with oil for a grain offering; ²⁶ one gold bowl

weighing four ounces, full of incense; [27] one young bull, one ram, and one male lamb a year old, for a burnt offering; [28] one male goat for a sin offering; [29] and two bulls, five rams, five male goats, and five male lambs a year old, for the fellowship sacrifice. This was the offering of Eliab son of Helon.

[30] On the fourth day Elizur son of Shedeur, leader of the Reubenites, presented an offering. [31] His offering was one silver dish weighing 3¼ pounds and one silver basin weighing 1¾ pounds, measured by the standard sanctuary shekel, both of them full of fine flour mixed with oil for a grain offering; [32] one gold bowl weighing four ounces, full of incense; [33] one young bull, one ram, and one male lamb a year old, for a burnt offering; [34] one male goat for a sin offering; [35] and two bulls, five rams, five male goats, and five male lambs a year old, for the fellowship sacrifice. This was the offering of Elizur son of Shedeur.

[36] On the fifth day Shelumiel son of Zurishaddai, leader of the Simeonites, presented an offering. [37] His offering was one silver dish weighing 3¼ pounds and one silver basin weighing 1¾ pounds, measured by the standard sanctuary shekel, both of them full of fine flour mixed with oil for a grain offering; [38] one gold bowl weighing four ounces, full of incense; [39] one young bull, one ram, and one male lamb a year old, for a burnt offering; [40] one male goat for a sin offering; [41] and two bulls, five rams, five male goats, and five male lambs a year old, for the fellowship sacrifice. This was the offering of Shelumiel son of Zurishaddai.

[42] On the sixth day Eliasaph son of Deuel, leader of the Gadites, presented an offering.

[43] His offering was one silver dish weighing 3¼ pounds and one silver basin weighing 1¾ pounds, measured by the standard sanctuary shekel, both of them full of fine flour mixed with oil for a grain offering; [44] one gold bowl weighing four ounces full of incense; [45] one young bull, one ram, and one male lamb a year old, for a burnt offering; [46] one male goat for a sin offering; [47] and two bulls, five rams, five male goats, and five male lambs a year old, for the fellowship sacrifice. This was the offering of Eliasaph son of Deuel.

[48] On the seventh day Elishama son of Ammihud, leader of the Ephraimites, presented an offering. [49] His offering was one silver dish weighing 3¼ pounds and one silver basin weighing 1¾ pounds, measured by the standard sanctuary shekel, both of them full of fine flour mixed with oil for a grain offering; [50] one gold bowl weighing four ounces, full of incense; [51] one young bull, one ram, and one male lamb a year old, for a burnt offering; [52] one male goat for a sin offering; [53] and two bulls, five rams, five male goats, and five male lambs a year old, for the fellowship sacrifice. This was the offering of Elishama son of Ammihud.

[54] On the eighth day Gamaliel son of Pedahzur, leader of the Manassites, presented an offering. [55] His offering was one silver dish weighing 3¼ pounds and one silver basin weighing 1¾ pounds, measured by the standard sanctuary shekel, both of them full of fine flour mixed with oil for a grain offering; [56] one gold bowl weighing four ounces, full of incense; [57] one young bull, one ram, and one male lamb a year old, for a burnt offering; [58] one male goat for a sin offering; [59] and two bulls, five rams, five male goats, and five male

lambs a year old, for the fellowship sacrifice. This was the offering of Gamaliel son of Pedahzur.

⁶⁰ On the ninth day Abidan son of Gideoni, leader of the Benjaminites, presented an offering. ⁶¹ His offering was one silver dish weighing 3¼ pounds and one silver basin weighing 1¾ pounds, measured by the standard sanctuary shekel, both of them full of fine flour mixed with oil for a grain offering; ⁶² one gold bowl weighing four ounces, full of incense; ⁶³ one young bull, one ram, and one male lamb a year old, for a burnt offering; ⁶⁴ one male goat for a sin offering; ⁶⁵ and two bulls, five rams, five male goats, and five male lambs a year old, for the fellowship sacrifice. This was the offering of Abidan son of Gideoni.

⁶⁶ On the tenth day Ahiezer son of Ammishaddai, leader of the Danites, presented an offering. ⁶⁷ His offering was one silver dish weighing 3¼ pounds and one silver basin weighing 1¾ pounds, measured by the standard sanctuary shekel, both of them full of fine flour mixed with oil for a grain offering; ⁶⁸ one gold bowl weighing four ounces, full of incense; ⁶⁹ one young bull, one ram, and one male lamb a year old, for a burnt offering; ⁷⁰ one male goat for a sin offering; ⁷¹ and two bulls, five rams, five male goats, and five male lambs a year old, for the fellowship sacrifice. This was the offering of Ahiezer son of Ammishaddai.

⁷² On the eleventh day Pagiel son of Ochran, leader of the Asherites, presented an offering. ⁷³ His offering was one silver dish weighing 3¼ pounds and one silver basin weighing 1¾ pounds, measured by the standard sanctuary shekel, both of them full of fine flour mixed with oil for a grain offering; ⁷⁴ one gold bowl weighing four ounces, full of incense; ⁷⁵ one young bull, one ram, and one male lamb a year old, for a burnt offering; ⁷⁶ one male goat for a sin offering; ⁷⁷ and two bulls, five rams,

five male goats, and five male lambs a year old, for the fellowship sacrifice. This was the offering of Pagiel son of Ochran.

[78] On the twelfth day Ahira son of Enan, leader of the Naphtalites, presented an offering. [79] His offering was one silver dish weighing 3¼ pounds and one silver basin weighing 1¾ pounds, measured by the standard sanctuary shekel, both of them full of fine flour mixed with oil for a grain offering; [80] one gold bowl weighing four ounces, full of incense; [81] one young bull, one ram, and one male lamb a year old, for a burnt offering; [82] one male goat for a sin offering; [83] and two bulls, five rams, five male goats, and five male lambs a year old, for the fellowship sacrifice. This was the offering of Ahira son of Enan.

[84] This was the dedication gift from the leaders of Israel for the altar when it was anointed: twelve silver dishes, twelve silver basins, and twelve gold bowls. [85] Each silver dish weighed 3¼ pounds, and each basin 1¾ pounds. The total weight of the silver articles was 60 pounds measured by the standard sanctuary shekel. [86] The twelve gold bowls full of incense each weighed four ounces measured by the standard sanctuary shekel. The total weight of the gold bowls was 3 pounds. [87] All the livestock for the burnt offering totaled twelve bulls, twelve rams, and twelve male lambs a year old, with their grain offerings, and twelve male goats for the sin offering. [88] All the livestock for the fellowship sacrifice totaled twenty-four bulls, sixty rams, sixty male goats, and sixty male lambs a year old. This was the dedication gift for the altar after it was anointed.

[89] When Moses entered the tent of meeting to speak with the Lord, he heard the voice speaking to him from above the mercy seat that was on the ark of the testimony, from between the two cherubim. He spoke to him that way.

40   NUMBERS: THE LORD GOES WITH US

DEUTERONOMY 12:5-7

⁵ Instead, turn to the place the LORD your God chooses from all your tribes to put his name for his dwelling and go there. ⁶ You are to bring there your burnt offerings and sacrifices, your tenths and personal contributions, your vow offerings and freewill offerings, and the firstborn of your herds and flocks. ⁷ You will eat there in the presence of the LORD your God and rejoice with your household in everything you do, because the LORD your God has blessed you.

ROMANS 12:1-2

A LIVING SACRIFICE

¹ Therefore, brothers and sisters, in view of the mercies of God, I urge you to present your bodies as a living sacrifice, holy and pleasing to God; this is your true worship. ² Do not be conformed to this age, but be transformed by the renewing of your mind, so that you may discern what is the good, pleasing, and perfect will of God.

WEEK 01 RESPONSE

Each week you'll have the opportunity to respond to your reading from the book of Numbers. Start by considering what you've read and observed in the text. Then, spend some time reflecting on how you've personally seen aspects of God's character as they are highlighted in Numbers.

OBSERVE

IN THIS WEEK'S READING, HOW DID YOU OBSERVE
GOD LEADING OR RESPONDING TO HIS PEOPLE?

HOW DID GOD'S PEOPLE RESPOND TO GOD OR HIS INSTRUCTION?

WHAT QUESTIONS DO YOU HAVE?

REFLECT

In God's responses and interactions with His people during their wilderness wandering, we see that God is loving, faithful, forgiving, and just through His responses and interactions with His people during their wilderness wandering. From discipline and consequences to affirmation and provision, the constancy of God's character remains. Where have you seen God's love, faithfulness, forgiveness, and/or justice around you this week?

LOVE	FAITHFULNESS

FORGIVENESS	JUSTICE

NUMBERS 14:18

THE LORD IS SLOW TO ANGER AND ABOUNDING IN FAITHFUL LOVE, FORGIVING INIQUITY AND REBELLION. BUT HE WILL NOT LEAVE THE GUILTY UNPUNISHED, BRINGING THE CONSEQUENCES OF THE FATHERS' INIQUITY ON THE CHILDREN TO THE THIRD AND FOURTH GENERATION.

© 2024 He Reads Truth. All rights reserved.

GRACE

Take this day to catch up on your reading,
pray, and rest in the presence of the Lord.

———

IF WE CONFESS OUR SINS,
HE IS FAITHFUL AND RIGHTEOUS
TO FORGIVE US OUR SINS AND
TO CLEANSE US FROM ALL
UNRIGHTEOUSNESS.

1 JOHN 1:9

DAY

WEEK

01

WEEKLY

Scripture is God-breathed and true. When we memorize it,
we carry His Word with us wherever we go.

For this reading plan, we will memorize our key verse,
Numbers 14:18. This week we will memorize the first
portion, a reminder of God's faithful love toward
His people.

——————

See tips for memorizing Scripture on page 180.

TRUTH

THE LORD IS SLOW TO ANGER AND ABOUNDING
IN FAITHFUL LOVE, FORGIVING INIQUITY AND
REBELLION. BUT HE WILL NOT LEAVE THE GUILTY
UNPUNISHED, BRINGING THE CONSEQUENCES OF
THE FATHERS' INIQUITY ON THE CHILDREN TO
THE THIRD AND FOURTH GENERATION.

NUMBERS 14:18

THE

DAY

SECOND

08

PASSOVER

THE LIGHTING IN THE TABERNACLE

[1] The LORD spoke to Moses: [2] "Speak to Aaron and tell him: When you set up the lamps, the seven lamps are to give light in front of the lampstand." [3] So Aaron did this; he set up its lamps to give light in front of the lampstand just as the LORD had commanded Moses. [4] This is the way the lampstand was made: it was a hammered work of gold, hammered from its base to its flower petals. The lampstand was made according to the pattern the LORD had shown Moses.

CONSECRATION OF THE LEVITES

[5] The LORD spoke to Moses: [6] "Take the Levites from among the Israelites and ceremonially cleanse them. [7] Do this to them for their purification: Sprinkle them with the purification water. Have them shave their entire bodies and wash their clothes, and so purify themselves.

[8] "They are to take a young bull and its grain offering of fine flour mixed with oil, and you are to take a second young bull for a sin offering. [9] Bring the Levites before the tent of meeting and assemble the entire Israelite community. [10] Then present the Levites before the LORD, and have the Israelites lay their hands on them. [11] Aaron is to present the Levites before the LORD as a presentation offering from the Israelites, so that they may perform the LORD's work. [12] Next the Levites are to lay their hands on the heads of the bulls. Sacrifice one as a sin offering and the other as a burnt offering to the LORD, to make atonement for the Levites.

[13] "You are to have the Levites stand before Aaron and his sons, and you are to present them before the LORD as a presentation offering. [14] In this way you are to separate the Levites from the rest of the Israelites so that the Levites will belong to me. [15] After that the Levites may come to serve at the tent of meeting, once you have ceremonially cleansed them and presented them as a presentation offering. [16] For they have been exclusively assigned to me from the Israelites. I have taken them for myself in place of all who come first from the womb, every Israelite firstborn. [17] For every firstborn among the Israelites is mine, both man and animal. I consecrated them to myself on the day I struck down every firstborn in the land of Egypt. [18] But I have taken the Levites in place of every firstborn among the Israelites. [19] From the Israelites, I have given the Levites exclusively to Aaron and his sons to perform the work for the Israelites at the tent of meeting and to make atonement on their behalf, so that no plague will come against the Israelites when they approach the sanctuary."

[20] Moses, Aaron, and the entire Israelite community did this to the Levites. The Israelites did everything to them the LORD commanded Moses regarding the Levites. [21] The Levites purified themselves and washed their clothes; then Aaron presented them before the LORD as a presentation offering. Aaron also made atonement for them to cleanse them ceremonially. [22] After that, the Levites came to do their work at the tent of meeting in the presence of Aaron and his sons. So they did to them as the LORD had commanded Moses concerning the Levites.

[23] The LORD spoke to Moses: [24] "In regard to the Levites: From twenty-five years old or more, a man enters the service in the work at the tent

———————————
———————————
———————————
———————————
———————————
———————————
———————————
———————————
———————————
———————————
———————————
———————————
———————————
———————————
———————————
———————————
———————————
———————————
———————————
———————————
———————————
———————————
———————————
———————————

of meeting. ²⁵ But at fifty years old he is to retire from his service in the work and no longer serve. ²⁶ He may assist his brothers to fulfill responsibilities at the tent of meeting, but he must not do the work. This is how you are to deal with the Levites regarding their duties."

NUMBERS 9:1-14

THE SECOND PASSOVER

¹ In the first month of the second year after their departure from the land of Egypt, the LORD told Moses in the Wilderness of Sinai, ² "The Israelites are to observe the Passover at its appointed time. ³ You must observe it at its appointed time on the fourteenth day of this month at twilight; you are to observe it according to all its statutes and ordinances." ⁴ So Moses told the Israelites to observe the Passover, ⁵ and they observed it in the first month on the fourteenth day at twilight in the Wilderness of Sinai. The Israelites did everything as the LORD had commanded Moses.

⁶ But there were some men who were unclean because of a human corpse, so they could not observe the Passover on that day. These men came before Moses and Aaron the same day ⁷ and said to him, "We are unclean because of a human corpse. Why should we be excluded from presenting the LORD's offering at its appointed time with the other Israelites?"

⁸ Moses replied to them, "Wait here until I hear what the LORD commands for you."

⁹ Then the LORD spoke to Moses: ¹⁰ "Tell the Israelites: When any one of you or your descendants is unclean because of a corpse or is on a distant journey, he may still observe the Passover to the LORD. ¹¹ Such people are to observe it in the second month, on the fourteenth day at twilight. They are to eat the animal with unleavened bread and bitter herbs; ¹² they may not leave any of it until morning or break any of its

bones. They must observe the Passover according to all its statutes.

¹³ "But the man who is ceremonially clean, is not on a journey, and yet fails to observe the Passover is to be cut off from his people, because he did not present the LORD's offering at its appointed time. That man will bear the consequences of his sin.

¹⁴ "If an alien resides with you and wants to observe the Passover to the LORD, he is to do it according to the Passover statute and its ordinances. You are to apply the same statute to both the resident alien and the native of the land."

🛡 GOING DEEPER

EXODUS 12:1–14

INSTRUCTIONS FOR THE PASSOVER

¹ The LORD said to Moses and Aaron in the land of Egypt, ² "This month is to be the beginning of months for you; it is the first month of your year. ³ Tell the whole community of Israel that on the tenth day of this month they must each select an animal of the flock according to their fathers' families, one animal per family. ⁴ If the household is too small for a whole animal, that person and the neighbor nearest his house are to select one based on the combined number of people; you should apportion the animal according to what each will eat. ⁵ You must have an unblemished animal, a year-old male; you may take it from either the sheep or the goats. ⁶ You are to keep it until the fourteenth day of this month; then the whole assembly of the community of Israel will slaughter the animals at twilight. ⁷ They must take some of the blood and put it on the two doorposts and the lintel of the houses where they eat them. ⁸ They are to eat the meat that night; they should eat it, roasted over the fire along with unleavened bread and bitter herbs. ⁹ Do not eat any of it raw or cooked

in boiling water, but only roasted over fire—its head as well as its legs and inner organs. [10] You must not leave any of it until morning; any part of it left until morning you must burn. [11] Here is how you must eat it: You must be dressed for travel, your sandals on your feet, and your staff in your hand. You are to eat it in a hurry; it is the LORD's Passover.

[12] "I will pass through the land of Egypt on that night and strike every firstborn male in the land of Egypt, both people and animals. I am the LORD; I will execute judgments against all the gods of Egypt. [13] The blood on the houses where you are staying will be a distinguishing mark for you; when I see the blood, I will pass over you. No plague will be among you to destroy you when I strike the land of Egypt.

[14] "THIS DAY IS TO BE A MEMORIAL FOR YOU, AND YOU MUST CELEBRATE IT AS A FESTIVAL TO THE LORD.

You are to celebrate it throughout your generations as a permanent statute."

1 CORINTHIANS 5:7-8

[7] Clean out the old leaven so that you may be a new unleavened batch, as indeed you are. For Christ our Passover lamb has been sacrificed. [8] Therefore, let us observe the feast, not with old leaven or with the leaven of malice and evil, but with the unleavened bread of sincerity and truth.

NOTES

GUIDANCE BY THE CLOUD

NUMBERS 9:15-23

GUIDANCE BY THE CLOUD

¹⁵ On the day the tabernacle was set up, the cloud covered the tabernacle, the tent of the testimony, and it appeared like fire above the tabernacle from evening until morning. ¹⁶ It remained that way continuously: the cloud would cover it, appearing like fire at night. ¹⁷ Whenever the cloud was lifted up above the tent, the Israelites would set out; at the place where the cloud stopped, there the Israelites camped. ¹⁸ At the LORD's command the Israelites set out, and at the LORD's command they camped. As long as the cloud stayed over the tabernacle, they camped.

¹⁹ Even when the cloud stayed over the tabernacle many days, the Israelites carried out the LORD's requirement and did not set out. ²⁰ Sometimes the cloud remained over the tabernacle for only a few days. They would camp at the LORD's command and set out at the LORD's command. ²¹ Sometimes the cloud remained only from evening until morning; when the cloud lifted in the morning, they set out. Or if it remained a day and a night, they moved out when the cloud lifted. ²² Whether it was two days, a month, or longer, the Israelites camped and did not set out as long as the cloud

> AT THE LORD'S COMMAND THE ISRAELITES SET OUT, AND AT THE LORD'S COMMAND THEY CAMPED. AS LONG AS THE CLOUD STAYED OVER THE TABERNACLE, THEY CAMPED.
>
> **NUMBERS 9:18**

stayed over the tabernacle. But when it was lifted, they set out. [23] They camped at the Lord's command, and they set out at the Lord's command. They carried out the Lord's requirement according to his command through Moses.

NUMBERS 10

TWO SILVER TRUMPETS

[1] The Lord spoke to Moses: [2] "Make two trumpets of hammered silver to summon the community and have the camps set out. [3] When both are sounded in long blasts, the entire community is to gather before you at the entrance to the tent of meeting. [4] However, if one is sounded, only the leaders, the heads of Israel's clans, are to gather before you.

[5] "When you sound short blasts, the camps pitched on the east are to set out. [6] When you sound short blasts a second time, the camps pitched on the south are to set out. Short blasts are to be sounded for them to set out. [7] When calling the assembly together, you are to sound long blasts, not short ones. [8] The sons of Aaron, the priests, are to sound the trumpets. Your use of these is a permanent statute throughout your generations.

[9] "When you enter into battle in your land against an adversary who is attacking you, sound short blasts on the trumpets, and you will be remembered before the Lord your God and be saved from your enemies. [10] You are to sound the trumpets over your burnt offerings and your fellowship sacrifices and on your joyous occasions, your appointed festivals, and the beginning of each of your months. They will serve as a reminder for you before your God: I am the Lord your God."

FROM SINAI TO PARAN

[11] During the second year, in the second month on the twentieth day of the month, the cloud was lifted up above the tabernacle of the testimony.

CLOUDS IN SCRIPTURE

God's presence is often represented by a cloud throughout Scripture, including when God used clouds to cover Mount Sinai as He gave Moses the law (Ex 19:9; 24:15–18), when a cloud shielded the disciples' eyes at Jesus's transfiguration (Mt 17:5), and when a cloud took Jesus into heaven at His ascension (Ac 1:9).

¹² **THE ISRAELITES TRAVELED ON FROM THE WILDERNESS OF SINAI, MOVING FROM ONE PLACE TO THE NEXT UNTIL THE CLOUD STOPPED IN THE WILDERNESS OF PARAN.**

¹³ They set out for the first time according to the LORD's command through Moses.

¹⁴ The military divisions of the camp of Judah's descendants with their banner set out first, and Nahshon son of Amminadab was over their divisions. ¹⁵ Nethanel son of Zuar was over the division of the tribe of Issachar's descendants, ¹⁶ and Eliab son of Helon was over the division of the tribe of Zebulun's descendants. ¹⁷ The tabernacle was then taken down, and the Gershonites and the Merarites set out, transporting the tabernacle.

¹⁸ The military divisions of the camp of Reuben with their banner set out, and Elizur son of Shedeur was over their divisions. ¹⁹ Shelumiel son of Zurishaddai was over the division of the tribe of Simeon's descendants, ²⁰ and Eliasaph son of Deuel was over the division of the tribe of Gad's descendants. ²¹ The Kohathites then set out, transporting the holy objects; the tabernacle was to be set up before their arrival.

²² Next the military divisions of the camp of Ephraim's descendants with their banner set out, and Elishama son of Ammihud was over their divisions. ²³ Gamaliel son of Pedahzur was over the division of the tribe of Manasseh's descendants, ²⁴ and Abidan son of Gideoni was over the division of the tribe of Benjamin's descendants.

²⁵ The military divisions of the camp of Dan's descendants with their banner set out, serving as rear guard for all the camps, and Ahiezer son of Ammishaddai was over their divisions. ²⁶ Pagiel son of Ochran was over the division of the tribe of Asher's descendants, ²⁷ and Ahira son of Enan was over the division of the tribe of Naphtali's descendants. ²⁸ This was the order of march for the Israelites by their military divisions as they set out.

²⁹ Moses said to Hobab, descendant of Reuel the Midianite and Moses's relative by marriage, "We're setting out for the place the LORD promised, 'I will give it to you.' Come with us, and we will treat you well, for the LORD has promised good things to Israel."

³⁰ But he replied to him, "I don't want to go. Instead, I will go to my own land and my relatives."

³¹ "Please don't leave us," Moses said, "since you know where we should camp in the wilderness, and you can serve as our eyes. ³² If you come with us, whatever good the LORD does for us we will do for you."

³³ They set out from the mountain of the LORD on a three-day journey with the ark of the LORD's covenant traveling ahead of them for those three days to seek a resting place for them. ³⁴ Meanwhile, the cloud of the LORD was over them by day when they set out from the camp.

³⁵ Whenever the ark set out, Moses would say:

Arise, LORD!
Let your enemies be scattered,
 and those who hate you flee from
  your presence.

36 When it came to rest, he would say:

Return, Lord,
to the countless thousands of Israel.

◆ GOING DEEPER

EXODUS 13:17-22

THE ROUTE OF THE EXODUS

17 When Pharaoh let the people go, God did not lead them along the road to the land of the Philistines, even though it was nearby; for God said, "The people will change their minds and return to Egypt if they face war." 18 So he led the people around toward the Red Sea along the road of the wilderness. And the Israelites left the land of Egypt in battle formation.

19 Moses took the bones of Joseph with him, because Joseph had made the Israelites swear a solemn oath, saying, "God will certainly come to your aid; then you must take my bones with you from this place."

20 They set out from Succoth and camped at Etham on the edge of the wilderness. 21 The Lord went ahead of them in a pillar of cloud to lead them on their way during the day and in a pillar of fire to give them light at night, so that they could travel day or night. 22 The pillar of cloud by day and the pillar of fire by night never left its place in front of the people.

PSALM 78:14

He led them with a cloud by day
and with a fiery light throughout the night.

COMPLAINTS ABOUT HARDSHIP

[1] Now the people began complaining openly before the LORD about hardship. When the LORD heard, his anger burned, and fire from the LORD blazed among them and consumed the outskirts of the camp. [2] Then the people cried out to Moses, and he prayed to the LORD, and the fire died down. [3] So that place was named Taberah, because the LORD's fire had blazed among them.

COMPLAINTS ABOUT FOOD

[4] The riffraff among them had a strong craving for other food. The Israelites wept again and said, "Who will feed us meat? [5] We remember the free fish we ate in Egypt, along with the cucumbers, melons, leeks, onions, and garlic.

[6] BUT NOW OUR APPETITE IS GONE; THERE'S NOTHING TO LOOK AT BUT THIS MANNA!"

[7] The manna resembled coriander seed, and its appearance was like that of bdellium. [8] The people walked around and gathered it. They ground it on a pair of grinding stones or crushed it in a mortar, then boiled it in a cooking pot and shaped it into cakes. It tasted like a pastry cooked with the finest oil. [9] When the dew fell on the camp at night, the manna would fall with it.

[10] Moses heard the people, family after family, weeping at the entrance of their tents. The LORD was very angry; Moses was also provoked. [11] So Moses asked the LORD, "Why have you brought such trouble on your servant? Why are you angry with me, and why do you burden me with all these people? [12] Did I conceive all these people? Did I give them birth so you should tell me, 'Carry them at your breast, as a nursing mother carries a baby,' to the land that you swore to give their ancestors? [13] Where can I get meat to give all these people? For they are weeping to me, 'Give us meat to eat!' [14] I can't carry all these people by myself. They are too much for me. [15] If you are going to treat me like this, please kill me

DAY 10

THE PEOPLE'S COMPLAINTS

right now if I have found favor with you, and don't let me see my misery anymore."

SEVENTY ELDERS ANOINTED

¹⁶ The Lord answered Moses, "Bring me seventy men from Israel known to you as elders and officers of the people. Take them to the tent of meeting and have them stand there with you. ¹⁷ Then I will come down and speak with you there. I will take some of the Spirit who is on you and put the Spirit on them. They will help you bear the burden of the people, so that you do not have to bear it by yourself.

¹⁸ "Tell the people: Consecrate yourselves in readiness for tomorrow, and you will eat meat because you wept in the Lord's hearing, 'Who will feed us meat? We were better off in Egypt.' The Lord will give you meat and you will eat. ¹⁹ You will eat, not for one day, or two days, or five days, or ten days, or twenty days, ²⁰ but for a whole month—until it comes out of your nostrils and becomes nauseating to you—because you have rejected the Lord who is among you, and wept before him, 'Why did we ever leave Egypt?'"

²¹ But Moses replied, "I'm in the middle of a people with six hundred thousand foot soldiers, yet you say, 'I will give them meat, and they will eat for a month.' ²² If flocks and herds were slaughtered for them, would they have enough? Or if all the fish in the sea were caught for them, would they have enough?"

²³ The Lord answered Moses, "Is the Lord's arm weak? Now you will see whether or not what I have promised will happen to you."

²⁴ Moses went out and told the people the words of the Lord. He brought seventy men from the elders of the people and had them stand around the tent. ²⁵ Then the Lord descended in the cloud and spoke to him. He took some of the Spirit who was on Moses and placed the Spirit on the seventy elders. As the

NOTES

Spirit rested on them, they prophesied, but they never did it again. [26] Two men had remained in the camp, one named Eldad and the other Medad; the Spirit rested on them—they were among those listed, but had not gone out to the tent—and they prophesied in the camp. [27] A young man ran and reported to Moses, "Eldad and Medad are prophesying in the camp."

[28] Joshua son of Nun, assistant to Moses since his youth, responded, "Moses, my lord, stop them!"

[29] But Moses asked him, "Are you jealous on my account? If only all the LORD's people were prophets and the LORD would place his Spirit on them!" [30] Then Moses returned to the camp along with the elders of Israel.

QUAIL IN THE CAMP

[31] A wind sent by the LORD came up and blew quail in from the sea; it dropped them all around the camp. They were flying three feet off the ground for about a day's journey in every direction. [32] The people were up all that day and night and all the next day gathering the quail—the one who took the least gathered sixty bushels—and they spread them out all around the camp.

[33] While the meat was still between their teeth, before it was chewed, the LORD's anger burned against the people, and the LORD struck them with a very severe plague. [34] So they named that place Kibroth-hattaavah, because there they buried the people who had craved the meat.

[35] From Kibroth-hattaavah the people moved on to Hazeroth and remained there.

♥ GOING DEEPER

EXODUS 16

MANNA AND QUAIL PROVIDED

[1] The entire Israelite community departed from Elim and came to the Wilderness of Sin, which is between Elim and Sinai, on the fifteenth day of the second month after they had left the land of Egypt. [2] The entire Israelite community grumbled against Moses and Aaron in the wilderness. [3] The Israelites said to them, "If only we had died by the LORD's hand in the land of Egypt, when we sat by pots of meat and ate all the bread we wanted. Instead, you brought us into this wilderness to make this whole assembly die of hunger!"

[4] Then the LORD said to Moses, "I am going to rain bread from heaven for you. The people are to go out each day and gather enough for that day. This way I will test them to see whether or not they will follow my instructions. [5] On the sixth day, when they prepare what they bring in, it will be twice as much as they gather on other days."

[6] So Moses and Aaron said to all the Israelites, "This evening you will know that it was the LORD who brought you out of the land of Egypt, [7] and in the morning you will see the LORD's glory because he has heard your complaints about him. For who are we that you complain about us?" [8] Moses continued, "The LORD will give you meat to eat this evening and all the bread you want in the morning, for he has heard the complaints that you are raising against him. Who are we? Your complaints are not against us but against the LORD."

⁹ Then Moses told Aaron, "Say to the entire Israelite community, 'Come before the LORD, for he has heard your complaints.'" ¹⁰ As Aaron was speaking to the entire Israelite community, they turned toward the wilderness, and there in a cloud the LORD's glory appeared.

¹¹ The LORD spoke to Moses, ¹² "I have heard the complaints of the Israelites. Tell them: At twilight you will eat meat, and in the morning you will eat bread until you are full. Then you will know that I am the LORD your God."

¹³ So at evening quail came and covered the camp. In the morning there was a layer of dew all around the camp. ¹⁴ When the layer of dew evaporated, there were fine flakes on the desert surface, as fine as frost on the ground. ¹⁵ When the Israelites saw it, they asked one another, "What is it?" because they didn't know what it was.

Moses told them, "It is the bread the LORD has given you to eat. ¹⁶ This is what the LORD has commanded: 'Gather as much of it as each person needs to eat. You may take two quarts per individual, according to the number of people each of you has in his tent.'"

¹⁷ So the Israelites did this. Some gathered a lot, some a little. ¹⁸ When they measured it by quarts, the person who gathered a lot had no surplus, and the person who gathered a little had no shortage. Each gathered as much as he needed to eat. ¹⁹ Moses said to them, "No one is to let any of it remain until morning." ²⁰ But they didn't listen to Moses; some people left part of it until morning, and it bred worms and stank. Therefore Moses was angry with them.

²¹ They gathered it every morning. Each gathered as much as he needed to eat, but when the sun grew hot, it

melted. [22] On the sixth day they gathered twice as much food, four quarts apiece, and all the leaders of the community came and reported this to Moses. [23] He told them, "This is what the LORD has said: 'Tomorrow is a day of complete rest, a holy Sabbath to the LORD. Bake what you want to bake, and boil what you want to boil, and set aside everything left over to be kept until morning.'"

[24] So they set it aside until morning as Moses commanded, and it didn't stink or have maggots in it. [25] "Eat it today," Moses said, "because today is a Sabbath to the LORD. Today you won't find any in the field. [26] For six days you will gather it, but on the seventh day, the Sabbath, there will be none."

[27] Yet on the seventh day some of the people went out to gather, but they did not find any. [28] Then the LORD said to Moses, "How long will you refuse to keep my commands and instructions? [29] Understand that the LORD has given you the Sabbath; therefore on the sixth day he will give you two days' worth of bread. Each of you stay where you are; no one is to leave his place on the seventh day." [30] So the people rested on the seventh day.

[31] The house of Israel named the substance manna. It resembled coriander seed, was white, and tasted like wafers made with honey. [32] Moses said, "This is what the LORD has commanded: 'Two quarts of it are to be preserved throughout your generations, so that they may see the bread I fed you in the wilderness when I brought you out of the land of Egypt.'"

[33] Moses told Aaron, "Take a container and put two quarts of manna in it. Then place it before the LORD to be preserved throughout your generations." [34] As the LORD commanded Moses, Aaron placed it before the testimony to be preserved.

[35] The Israelites ate manna for forty years, until they came to an inhabited land. They ate manna until they reached the border of the land of Canaan. [36] (They used a measure called an omer, which held two quarts.)

PSALM 78:17–20

[17] But they continued to sin against him,
rebelling in the desert against the Most High.
[18] They deliberately tested God,
demanding the food they craved.
[19] They spoke against God, saying,
"Is God able to provide food in the wilderness?
[20] Look! He struck the rock and water
   gushed out;
torrents overflowed.
But can he also provide bread
or furnish meat for his people?"

PHILIPPIANS 2:14–15

[14] DO EVERYTHING WITHOUT GRUMBLING AND ARGUING,

[15] so that you may be blameless and pure, children of God who are faultless in a crooked and perverted generation, among whom you shine like stars in the world...

NOTES

MIRIAM AND AARON REBEL AGAINST MOSES

"I SPEAK WITH HIM DIRECTLY,
OPENLY, AND NOT IN RIDDLES;
HE SEES THE FORM OF THE LORD.
SO WHY WERE YOU NOT AFRAID TO
SPEAK AGAINST MY SERVANT MOSES?"

NUMBERS 12:8

NUMBERS 12

MIRIAM AND AARON REBEL

[1] Miriam and Aaron criticized Moses because of the Cushite woman he married (for he had married a Cushite woman). [2] They said, "Does the LORD speak only through Moses? Does he not also speak through us?" And the LORD heard it. [3] Moses was a very humble man, more so than anyone on the face of the earth.

[4] Suddenly the LORD said to Moses, Aaron, and Miriam, "You three come out to the tent of meeting." So the three of them went out. [5] Then the LORD descended in a pillar of cloud, stood at the entrance to the tent, and summoned Aaron and Miriam. When the two of them came forward, [6] he said:

"Listen to what I say:
If there is a prophet among you from the LORD,
I make myself known to him in a vision;
I speak with him in a dream.
[7] Not so with my servant Moses;
he is faithful in all my household.
[8] I speak with him directly,
openly, and not in riddles;
he sees the form of the LORD.

So why were you not afraid to speak against my servant Moses?" [9] The LORD's anger burned against them, and he left.

[10] As the cloud moved away from the tent, Miriam's skin suddenly became diseased, resembling snow. When Aaron turned toward her, he saw that she was diseased [11] and said to Moses, "My lord, please don't hold against us this sin we have so foolishly committed. [12] Please don't let her be like a dead baby whose flesh is half eaten away when he comes out of his mother's womb."

[13] Then Moses cried out to the LORD, "God, please heal her!"

[14] The LORD answered Moses, "If her father had merely spit in her face, wouldn't she remain in disgrace for seven days? Let her be confined outside the camp for seven days; after that she may be brought back in." [15] So Miriam was confined outside the camp for seven days, and the people did not move on until Miriam was brought back in. [16] After that, the people set out from Hazeroth and camped in the Wilderness of Paran.

◆ GOING DEEPER

ACTS 3:22-26

[22] Moses said: The Lord your God will raise up for you a prophet like me from among your brothers. You must listen to everything he tells you. [23] And everyone who does not listen to that prophet will be completely cut off from the people.

[24] In addition, all the prophets who have spoken, from Samuel and those after him, have also foretold these days. [25] You are the sons of the prophets and of the covenant that God made with your ancestors, saying to Abraham, And all the families of the earth will be blessed through your offspring. [26] God raised up his servant and sent him first to you to bless you by turning each of you from your evil ways.

HEBREWS 3:1-6

OUR APOSTLE AND HIGH PRIEST

[1] Therefore, holy brothers and sisters, who share in a heavenly calling, consider Jesus, the apostle and high priest of our confession. [2] He was faithful to the one who appointed him, just as Moses was in all God's household. [3] For Jesus is considered worthy of more glory than Moses, just as the builder has more honor than the house. [4] Now every house is built by someone, but the one who built everything is God. [5] Moses was faithful as a servant in all God's household, as a testimony to what would be said in the future. [6] But Christ was faithful as a Son over his household. And we are that household if we hold on to our confidence and the hope in which we boast.

NOTES

TYPES OF WRITING IN NUMBERS

Knowing the type of literature we're reading helps us better understand how to engage with it, keeping in mind the context, meaning, and intent of the original text. The author of Numbers wove many literary devices together when recording Israel's trek to the promised land. Each literary device serves a different purpose, highlighting different aspects of the wilderness journey. Here is a brief overview of these different types of writing, along with an example of where you can find each one in the book of Numbers.

(1) CENSUS

The Lord directed Moses to take a census on multiple occasions in the book of Numbers. Each census was conducted for a specific purpose, ranging from determining military eligibility to tabernacle responsibilities and land allotments. Keep in mind, ancient census data, such as what we find in Numbers, was not gathered to represent every individual or provide a complete picture of a nation.

EXAMPLE: NUMBERS 1:1–46

(2) LAW

The laws found within the book of Numbers, along with the rest of the laws in the Pentateuch (for more on the Pentateuch, turn to page 14), helped to shape Israel's developing identity as the people of God. The law spoke to the social, political, religious, economic, and judicial aspects of an ancient society that had not yet developed the infrastructures characteristic of modern societies. As you read Numbers, keep in mind that these laws were created during the old covenant, but as readers today we live under the new covenant where the law has been fulfilled in Christ.

EXAMPLE: NUMBERS 5:5–10

(3)

NARRATIVE

————

The narratives in Numbers are true accounts of events during Israel's years in the wilderness. These narratives serve as theological history, written to show how God worked in and through this trying time in Israel's story. This genre records and describes the experiences of God's people and God's interactions with them, but contains nuances, perspectives, and dialogue that law and census do not account for.

EXAMPLE: NUMBERS 13

(4)

PROPHETIC POETRY

————

In Numbers, the seer Balaam is hired by the king of Moab to place a curse on the nation of Israel. Chapters 23 and 24 record the Lord intervening and speaking blessing through Balaam, in the literary style of prophetic poetry. These four oracles, each with a repeated structure, affirm God's ongoing, promised blessing for the nation of Israel.

EXAMPLE: NUMBERS 23:7–10

© 2024 He Reads Truth. All rights reserved.

SCOUTING

DAY   OUT   12

CANAAN

NUMBERS 13

SCOUTING OUT CANAAN

¹ The Lord spoke to Moses: ² "Send men to scout out the land of Canaan I am giving to the Israelites. Send one man who is a leader among them from each of their ancestral tribes." ³ Moses sent them from the Wilderness of Paran at the Lord's command. All the men were leaders in Israel. ⁴ These were their names:

Shammua son of Zaccur from the tribe of Reuben;
⁵ Shaphat son of Hori from the tribe of Simeon;
⁶ Caleb son of Jephunneh from the tribe of Judah;
⁷ Igal son of Joseph from the tribe of Issachar;
⁸ Hoshea son of Nun from the tribe of Ephraim;
⁹ Palti son of Raphu from the tribe of Benjamin;
¹⁰ Gaddiel son of Sodi from the tribe of Zebulun;
¹¹ Gaddi son of Susi from the tribe of Manasseh
   (from the tribe of Joseph);
¹² Ammiel son of Gemalli from the tribe of Dan;
¹³ Sethur son of Michael from the tribe of Asher;
¹⁴ Nahbi son of Vophsi from the tribe of Naphtali;
¹⁵ Geuel son of Machi from the tribe of Gad.

¹⁶ These were the names of the men Moses sent to scout out the land, and Moses renamed Hoshea son of Nun, Joshua.

¹⁷ When Moses sent them to scout out the land of Canaan, he told them, "Go up this way to the Negev, then go up into the hill country. ¹⁸ See what the land is like, and whether the people who live there are strong or weak, few or many. ¹⁹ Is the land they live in good or bad? Are the cities they live in encampments or fortifications? ²⁰ Is the land fertile or unproductive? Are there trees in it or not? Be courageous. Bring back some fruit from the land." It was the season for the first ripe grapes.

²¹ So they went up and scouted out the land from the Wilderness of Zin as far as Rehob near the entrance

ISRAEL'S WILDERNESS NEIGHBORS

The Israelites encountered many different people groups as they traveled through the wilderness. As you read, these brief backgrounds highlight the history of some of the tribes surrounding the borders of the promised land.

CANAANITES

The descendants of Canaan, the grandson of Noah. Smaller tribes included Jebusites, Amorites, Hethites, and the Zemarites, but tribes in the geographical region of Canaan were also collectively called Canaanites.

to Hamath. ²² They went up through the Negev and came to Hebron, where Ahiman, Sheshai, and Talmai, the descendants of Anak, were living. Hebron was built seven years before Zoan in Egypt. ²³ When they came to Eshcol Valley, they cut down a branch with a single cluster of grapes, which was carried on a pole by two men. They also took some pomegranates and figs. ²⁴ That place was called Eshcol Valley because of the cluster of grapes the Israelites cut there. ²⁵ At the end of forty days they returned from scouting out the land.

REPORT ABOUT CANAAN

²⁶ The men went back to Moses, Aaron, and the entire Israelite community in the Wilderness of Paran at Kadesh. They brought back a report for them and the whole community, and they showed them the fruit of the land. ²⁷ They reported to Moses, "We went into the land where you sent us. Indeed it is flowing with milk and honey, and here is some of its fruit. ²⁸ However, the people living in the land are strong, and the cities are large and fortified. We also saw the descendants of Anak there. ²⁹ The Amalekites are living in the land of the Negev; the Hethites, Jebusites, and Amorites live in the hill country; and the **Canaanites** live by the sea and along the Jordan."

³⁰ Then Caleb quieted the people in the presence of Moses and said, "Let's go up now and take possession of the land because we can certainly conquer it!"

³¹ But the men who had gone up with him responded, "We can't attack the people because they are stronger than we are!" ³² So they gave a negative report to the Israelites about the land they had scouted: "The land we passed through to explore is one that devours its inhabitants, and all the people we saw in it are men of great size. ³³ We even saw the Nephilim there—the descendants of Anak come from the Nephilim! To

ourselves we seemed like grasshoppers, and we must have seemed the same to them."

◆ GOING DEEPER

EXODUS 3:8, 17

8 "...and I have come down to rescue them from the power of the Egyptians and to bring them from that land to a good and spacious land, a land flowing with milk and honey—the territory of the Canaanites, Hethites, Amorites, Perizzites, Hivites, and Jebusites."

...

17 "AND I HAVE PROMISED YOU THAT I WILL BRING YOU UP FROM THE MISERY OF EGYPT TO THE LAND OF THE CANAANITES, HETHITES, AMORITES, PERIZZITES, HIVITES, AND JEBUSITES—A LAND FLOWING WITH MILK AND HONEY."

MATTHEW 8:23-27

WIND AND WAVES OBEY JESUS

23 As he got into the boat, his disciples followed him. 24 Suddenly, a violent storm arose on the sea, so that the boat was being swamped by the waves—but Jesus kept sleeping. 25 So the disciples came and woke him up, saying, "Lord, save us! We're going to die!"

26 He said to them, "Why are you afraid, you of little faith?" Then he got up and rebuked the winds and the sea, and there was a great calm.

27 The men were amazed and asked, "What kind of man is this? Even the winds and the sea obey him!"

WEEK 02 RESPONSE

OBSERVE

IN THIS WEEK'S READING, HOW DID YOU OBSERVE
GOD LEADING OR RESPONDING TO HIS PEOPLE?

HOW DID GOD'S PEOPLE RESPOND TO GOD OR HIS INSTRUCTION?

WHAT QUESTIONS DO YOU HAVE?

REFLECT

Where have you seen God's love, faithfulness, forgiveness, and/or justice around you this week?

LOVE	FAITHFULNESS

FORGIVENESS	JUSTICE

NUMBERS 14:18

THE LORD IS SLOW TO ANGER AND ABOUNDING IN FAITHFUL LOVE, FORGIVING INIQUITY AND REBELLION. BUT HE WILL NOT LEAVE THE GUILTY UNPUNISHED, BRINGING THE CONSEQUENCES OF THE FATHERS' INIQUITY ON THE CHILDREN TO THE THIRD AND FOURTH GENERATION.

© 2024 He Reads Truth. All rights reserved.

DAY
13

GRACE

Take this day to catch up on your reading,
pray, and rest in the presence of the Lord.

————

HE LED THEM WITH A CLOUD BY
DAY AND WITH A FIERY LIGHT
THROUGHOUT THE NIGHT.

PSALM 78:14

DAY

WEEK
02

Scripture is God-breathed and true. When we memorize it,
we carry His Word with us wherever we go.

We are continuing to memorize our key verse, Numbers 14:18.
This week we will add the next section, showing how God
demonstrates His love through forgiveness.

———

See tips for memorizing Scripture on page 180.

TRUTH

THE LORD IS SLOW TO ANGER AND ABOUNDING
IN FAITHFUL LOVE, FORGIVING INIQUITY AND
REBELLION. BUT HE WILL NOT LEAVE THE GUILTY
UNPUNISHED, BRINGING THE CONSEQUENCES OF
THE FATHERS' INIQUITY ON THE CHILDREN TO
THE THIRD AND FOURTH GENERATION.

NUMBERS 14:18

GOD'S JUDGMENT OF ISRAEL'S REBELLION

———

"NONE OF THE MEN WHO HAVE
SEEN MY GLORY AND THE SIGNS I
PERFORMED IN EGYPT AND IN THE
WILDERNESS, AND HAVE TESTED
ME THESE TEN TIMES AND DID NOT
OBEY ME, WILL EVER SEE THE LAND I
SWORE TO GIVE THEIR ANCESTORS."

NUMBERS 14:22–23

NUMBERS 14

ISRAEL'S REFUSAL TO ENTER CANAAN

¹ Then the whole community broke into loud cries, and the people wept that night. ² All the Israelites complained about Moses and Aaron, and the whole community told them, "If only we had died in the land of Egypt, or if only we had died in this wilderness! ³ Why is the LORD bringing us into this land to die by the sword? Our wives and children will become plunder. Wouldn't it be better for us to go back to Egypt?" ⁴ So they said to one another, "Let's appoint a leader and go back to Egypt."

⁵ Then Moses and Aaron fell facedown in front of the whole assembly of the Israelite community. ⁶ Joshua son of Nun and Caleb son of Jephunneh, who were among those who scouted out the land, tore their clothes ⁷ and said to the entire Israelite community, "The land we passed through and explored is an extremely good land. ⁸ If the LORD is pleased with us, he will bring us into this land, a land flowing with milk and honey, and give it to us. ⁹ Only don't rebel against the LORD, and don't be afraid of the people of the land, for we will devour them. Their protection has been removed from them, and the LORD is with us. Don't be afraid of them!"

¹⁰ While the whole community threatened to stone them, the glory of the LORD appeared to all the Israelites at the tent of meeting.

GOD'S JUDGMENT OF ISRAEL'S REBELLION

¹¹ The LORD said to Moses,

"HOW LONG WILL THESE PEOPLE DESPISE ME? HOW LONG WILL THEY NOT TRUST IN ME DESPITE ALL THE SIGNS I HAVE PERFORMED AMONG THEM?

THE WILDERNESS IN SCRIPTURE

Physically, the wilderness regions of the ancient Middle East were uninhabited or undeveloped lands. For Israel, their time in the wilderness was one of physical and spiritual wandering that several biblical authors recall to remind their audiences of the effects of Israel's rebellion and doubt about God's faithfulness (Neh 9:19–21; Ps 78:40; 95:8; Ezk 20:13–25; Ac 7:44; 13:18; 1Co 10:5; Heb 3:8, 17).

Many of the psalmists and prophets used the wilderness to symbolize seasons of spiritual wandering, while images of blossoming in the wilderness described the hope of God cleansing His people of their sin (Ps 55:7; 78:52; Is 32:15–16; 40:3–4; 43:19; 51:3; Hs 2:14–15).

ISRAEL'S WILDERNESS NEIGHBORS

AMALEKITES
A tribe that occupied the southern border of the promised land. Amalek, their ancestor, was mentioned in one of Balaam's oracles (Nm 24:20).

[12] I will strike them with a plague and destroy them. Then I will make you into a greater and mightier nation than they are."

[13] But Moses replied to the LORD, "The Egyptians will hear about it, for by your strength you brought up this people from them. [14] They will tell it to the inhabitants of this land. They have heard that you, LORD, are among these people, how you, LORD, are seen face to face, how your cloud stands over them, and how you go before them in a pillar of cloud by day and in a pillar of fire by night. [15] If you kill this people with a single blow, the nations that have heard of your fame will declare, [16] 'Since the LORD wasn't able to bring this people into the land he swore to give them, he has slaughtered them in the wilderness.'

[17] "So now, may my Lord's power be magnified just as you have spoken: [18] The LORD is slow to anger and abounding in faithful love, forgiving iniquity and rebellion. But he will not leave the guilty unpunished, bringing the consequences of the fathers' iniquity on the children to the third and fourth generation. [19] Please pardon the iniquity of this people, in keeping with the greatness of your faithful love, just as you have forgiven them from Egypt until now."

[20] The LORD responded, "I have pardoned them as you requested. [21] Yet as I live and as the whole earth is filled with the LORD's glory, [22] none of the men who have seen my glory and the signs I performed in Egypt and in the wilderness, and have tested me these ten times and did not obey me, [23] will ever see the land I swore to give their ancestors. None of those who have despised me will see it. [24] But since my servant Caleb has a different spirit and has remained loyal to me, I will bring him into the land where he has gone, and his descendants will inherit it. [25] Since the **Amalekites** and Canaanites are living in the lowlands, turn back tomorrow and head for the wilderness in the direction of the Red Sea."

26 Then the LORD spoke to Moses and Aaron: 27 "How long must I endure this evil community that keeps complaining about me? I have heard the Israelites' complaints that they make against me. 28 Tell them: As I live—this is the LORD's declaration—I will do to you exactly as I heard you say. 29 Your corpses will fall in this wilderness—all of you who were registered in the census, the entire number of you twenty years old or more—because you have complained about me. 30 I swear that none of you will enter the land I promised to settle you in, except Caleb son of Jephunneh and Joshua son of Nun. 31 I will bring your children whom you said would become plunder into the land you rejected, and they will enjoy it. 32 But as for you, your corpses will fall in this wilderness. 33 Your children will be shepherds in the wilderness for forty years and bear the penalty for your acts of unfaithfulness until all your corpses lie scattered in the wilderness. 34 You will bear the consequences of your iniquities forty years based on the number of the forty days that you scouted the land, a year for each day. You will know my displeasure. 35 I, the LORD, have spoken. I swear that I will do this to the entire evil community that has conspired against me. They will come to an end in the wilderness, and there they will die."

36 So the men Moses sent to scout out the land, and who returned and incited the entire community to complain about him by spreading a negative report about the land— 37 those men who spread the negative report about the land were struck down by the LORD. 38 Only Joshua son of Nun and Caleb son of Jephunneh remained alive of those men who went to scout out the land.

ISRAEL ROUTED

39 When Moses reported these words to all the Israelites, the people were overcome with grief. 40 They got up early the next morning and went up the ridge of

the hill country, saying, "Let's go to the place the LORD promised, for we were wrong."

[41] But Moses responded, "Why are you going against the LORD's command? It won't succeed. [42] Don't go, because the LORD is not among you and you will be defeated by your enemies. [43] The Amalekites and Canaanites are right in front of you, and you will fall by the sword. The LORD won't be with you, since you have turned from following him."

[44] But they dared to go up the ridge of the hill country, even though the ark of the LORD's covenant and Moses did not leave the camp. [45] Then the Amalekites and Canaanites who lived in that part of the hill country came down, attacked them, and routed them as far as Hormah.

🔖 GOING DEEPER

PSALM 106:24-27

[24] They despised the pleasant land
and did not believe his promise.
[25] They grumbled in their tents
and did not listen to the LORD.
[26] So he raised his hand against them with
      an oath
that he would make them fall in the desert
[27] and would disperse their descendants
among the nations,
scattering them throughout the lands.

EZEKIEL 20:10-20

[10] "So I brought them out of the land of Egypt and led them into the wilderness. [11] Then I gave them my statutes and explained my ordinances to them—the person who does them will live by them. [12] I also gave them my Sabbaths to serve as a sign between me and them, so that they would know that I am the LORD who consecrates them.

[13] "But the house of Israel rebelled against me in the wilderness. They did not follow my statutes and they rejected my ordinances—the person who does them will live by them. They also completely profaned my Sabbaths. So I considered pouring out my wrath on them in the wilderness to put an end to them. [14] But I acted for the sake of my name, so that it would not be profaned in the eyes of the nations in whose sight I had brought them out. [15] However, I swore to them in the wilderness that I would not bring them into the land I had given them—the most beautiful of all lands, flowing with milk and honey— [16] because they rejected my ordinances, profaned my Sabbaths, and did not follow my statutes. For their hearts went after their idols. [17] Yet

I spared them from destruction and did not bring them to an end in the wilderness.

18 "THEN I SAID TO THEIR CHILDREN IN THE WILDERNESS, 'DON'T FOLLOW THE STATUTES OF YOUR FATHERS, DEFILE YOURSELVES WITH THEIR IDOLS, OR KEEP THEIR ORDINANCES.

19 I am the LORD your God. Follow my statutes, keep my ordinances, and practice them. 20 Keep my Sabbaths holy, and they will be a sign between me and you, so you may know that I am the LORD your God.'"

HEBREWS 3:15-19

15 As it is said:

Today, if you hear his voice,
    do not harden your hearts as in the rebellion.

16 For who heard and rebelled? Wasn't it all who came out of Egypt under Moses? 17 With whom was God angry for forty years? Wasn't it with those who sinned, whose bodies fell in the wilderness? 18 And to whom did he swear that they would not enter his rest, if not to those who disobeyed? 19 So we see that they were unable to enter because of unbelief.

REMEMBERING AND OBEYING GOD'S COMMANDS

NUMBERS 15

LAWS ABOUT OFFERINGS

[1] The LORD instructed Moses, [2] "Speak to the Israelites and tell them: When you enter the land I am giving you to settle in, [3] and you make a food offering to the LORD from the herd or flock—either a burnt offering or a sacrifice, to fulfill a vow, or as a freewill offering, or at your appointed festivals—to produce a pleasing aroma for the LORD, [4] the one presenting his offering to the LORD is also to present a grain offering of two quarts of fine flour mixed with a quart of oil. [5] Prepare a quart of wine as a drink offering with the burnt offering or sacrifice of each lamb.

[6] "If you prepare a grain offering with a ram, it is to be four quarts of fine flour mixed with a third of a gallon of oil. [7] Also present a third of a gallon of wine for a drink offering as a pleasing aroma to the LORD.

[8] "If you prepare a young bull as a burnt offering or as a sacrifice, to fulfill a vow, or as a fellowship offering to the LORD, [9] a grain offering of six quarts of fine flour mixed with two quarts of oil is to be presented with the bull. [10] Also present two quarts of wine as a drink offering. It is a food offering, a pleasing aroma to the LORD. [11] This is to be done for each ox, ram, lamb, or goat. [12] This is how you are to prepare each of them, no matter how many.

[13] "Every Israelite is to prepare these things in this way when he presents a food offering as a pleasing aroma to the LORD. [14] When an alien

resides with you or someone else is among you and wants to prepare a food offering as a pleasing aroma to the Lord, he is to do exactly as you do throughout your generations. ¹⁵ The assembly is to have the same statute for both you and the resident alien as a permanent statute throughout your generations. You and the alien will be alike before the Lord. ¹⁶ The same law and the same ordinance will apply to both you and the alien who resides with you."

¹⁷ The Lord instructed Moses, ¹⁸ "Speak to the Israelites and tell them: After you enter the land where I am bringing you, ¹⁹ you are to offer a contribution to the Lord when you eat from the food of the land. ²⁰ You are to offer a loaf from your first batch of dough as a contribution; offer it just like a contribution from the threshing floor. ²¹ Throughout your generations, you are to give the Lord a contribution from the first batch of your dough.

²² "When you sin unintentionally and do not obey all these commands that the Lord spoke to Moses— ²³ all that the Lord has commanded you through Moses, from the day the Lord issued the commands and onward throughout your generations— ²⁴ and if it was done unintentionally without the community's awareness, the entire community is to prepare one young bull for a burnt offering as a pleasing aroma to the Lord, with its grain offering and drink offering according to the regulation, and one male goat as a sin offering. ²⁵ The priest will then make atonement for the entire Israelite community so that they may be forgiven, for the sin was unintentional. They are to bring their offering, a food offering to the Lord, and their sin offering before the Lord for their unintentional sin. ²⁶ The entire Israelite community and the alien who resides among them will be forgiven, since it happened to all the people unintentionally.

27 "If one person sins unintentionally, he is to present a year-old female goat as a sin offering. 28 The priest will then make atonement before the Lord on behalf of the person who acts in error sinning unintentionally, and when he makes atonement for him, he will be forgiven. 29 You are to have the same law for the person who acts in error, whether he is an Israelite or an alien who resides among you.

30 "But the person who acts defiantly, whether native or resident alien, blasphemes the Lord. That person is to be cut off from his people. 31 He will certainly be cut off, because he has despised the Lord's word and broken his command; his guilt remains on him."

SABBATH VIOLATION

32 While the Israelites were in the wilderness, they found a man gathering wood on the Sabbath day. 33 Those who found him gathering wood brought him to Moses, Aaron, and the entire community. 34 They placed him in custody because it had not been decided what should be done to him. 35 Then the Lord told Moses, "The man is to be put to death. The entire community is to stone him outside the camp." 36 So the entire community brought him outside the camp and stoned him to death, as the Lord had commanded Moses.

[37] The LORD said to Moses, [38] "Speak to the Israelites and tell them that throughout their generations they are to make tassels for the corners of their garments, and put a blue cord on the tassel at each corner. [39] These will serve as tassels for you to look at, so that you may remember all the LORD's commands and obey them and not prostitute yourselves by following your own heart and your own eyes. [40] This way you will remember and obey all my commands and be holy to your God. [41] I am the LORD your God who brought you out of the land of Egypt to be your God; I am the LORD your God."

GOING DEEPER

LEVITICUS 20:26

"You are to be holy to me because I, the Lord, am holy, and I have set you apart from the nations to be mine."

1 PETER 1:15–16

[15] But as the one who called you is holy, you also are to be holy in all your conduct; [16] for it is written, Be holy, because I am holy.

KORAH INCITES REBELLION AGAINST MOSES

NUMBERS 16

KORAH INCITES REBELLION

¹ Now Korah son of Izhar, son of Kohath, son of Levi, with Dathan and Abiram, sons of Eliab, and On son of Peleth, sons of Reuben, took ² two hundred fifty prominent Israelite men who were leaders of the community and representatives in the assembly, and they rebelled against Moses. ³ They came together against Moses and Aaron and told them, "You have gone too far! Everyone in the entire community is holy, and the LORD is among them. Why then do you exalt yourselves above the LORD's assembly?"

⁴ When Moses heard this, he fell facedown. ⁵ Then he said to Korah and all his followers, "Tomorrow morning the LORD will reveal who belongs to him, who is set apart, and the one he will let come near him. He will let the one he chooses come near him. ⁶ Korah, you and all your followers are to do this: take firepans, and tomorrow ⁷ place fire in them and put incense on them before the LORD. Then the man the LORD chooses will be the one who is set apart. It is you Levites who have gone too far!"

⁸ Moses also told Korah, "Now listen, Levites! ⁹ Isn't it enough for you that the God of Israel has separated you from the Israelite community to bring you near to himself, to perform the work at the LORD's tabernacle, and to stand before the community to minister to them? ¹⁰ He has brought you near, and all your fellow Levites who are with you, but you are pursuing the priesthood as well. ¹¹ Therefore, it is you

THE LORD WILL REVEAL WHO BELONGS TO HIM, WHO IS SET APART, AND THE ONE HE WILL LET COME NEAR HIM.

NUMBERS 16:5

_____

_____

_____

_____

_____

_____

_____

_____

_____

_____

_____

_____

_____

_____

_____

_____

_____

_____

_____

_____

_____

_____

and all your followers who have conspired against the LORD! As for Aaron, who is he that you should complain about him?"

¹² Moses sent for Dathan and Abiram, the sons of Eliab, but they said, "We will not come! ¹³ Is it not enough that you brought us up from a land flowing with milk and honey to kill us in the wilderness? Do you also have to appoint yourself as ruler over us? ¹⁴ Furthermore, you didn't bring us to a land flowing with milk and honey or give us an inheritance of fields and vineyards. Will you gouge out the eyes of these men? We will not come!"

¹⁵ Then Moses became angry and said to the LORD, "Don't respect their offering. I have not taken one donkey from them or mistreated a single one of them." ¹⁶ So Moses told Korah, "You and all your followers are to appear before the LORD tomorrow—you, they, and Aaron. ¹⁷ Each of you is to take his firepan, place incense on it, and present his firepan before the LORD—250 firepans. You and Aaron are each to present your firepan also."

¹⁸ Each man took his firepan, placed fire in it, put incense on it, and stood at the entrance to the tent of meeting along with Moses and Aaron. ¹⁹ After Korah assembled the whole community against them at the entrance to the tent of meeting, the glory of the LORD appeared to the whole community. ²⁰ The LORD spoke to Moses and Aaron, ²¹ "Separate yourselves from this community so I may consume them instantly."

²² But Moses and Aaron fell facedown and said, "God, God who gives breath to all, when one man sins, will you vent your wrath on the whole community?"

²³ The LORD replied to Moses, ²⁴ "Tell the community: Get away from the dwellings of Korah, Dathan, and Abiram."

²⁵ Moses got up and went to Dathan and Abiram, and the elders of Israel followed him. ²⁶ He warned the community, "Get away now from the tents of these wicked men. Don't touch anything that belongs to them, or you will be swept away because of all their sins." ²⁷ So they got away from the dwellings of Korah, Dathan, and Abiram. Meanwhile, Dathan and Abiram came out and stood at the entrance of their tents with their wives, children, and infants.

²⁸ Then Moses said, "This is how you will know that the LORD sent me to do all these things and that it was not of my own will: ²⁹ If these men die naturally as all people would, and suffer the fate of all, then the LORD has not sent me. ³⁰ But if the LORD brings about something unprecedented, and the ground opens its mouth and swallows them along with all that belongs to them so that they go down alive into Sheol, then you will know that these men have despised the LORD."

³¹ Just as he finished speaking all these words, the ground beneath them split open. ³² The earth opened its mouth and swallowed them and their households, all Korah's people, and all their possessions. ³³ They went down alive into Sheol with all that belonged to them. The earth closed over them, and they vanished from the assembly. ³⁴ At their cries, all the people of Israel who were around them fled because they thought, "The earth may swallow us too!" ³⁵ Fire also came out from the LORD and consumed the 250 men who were presenting the incense.

³⁶ Then the LORD spoke to Moses: ³⁷ "Tell Eleazar son of Aaron the priest to remove the firepans from the burning debris, because they are holy, and scatter the fire far away. ³⁸ As for the firepans of those who sinned at the cost of their own lives, make them into hammered sheets as plating for the altar, for they presented them before the LORD, and the firepans are holy. They will be a sign to the Israelites."

NOTES

³⁹ So the priest Eleazar took the bronze firepans that those who were burned had presented, and they were hammered into plating for the altar, ⁴⁰ just as the LORD commanded him through Moses. It was to be a reminder for the Israelites that no unauthorized person outside the lineage of Aaron should approach to offer incense before the LORD and become like Korah and his followers.

⁴¹ The next day the entire Israelite community complained about Moses and Aaron, saying, "You have killed the LORD's people!" ⁴² When the community assembled against them, Moses and Aaron turned toward the tent of meeting, and suddenly the cloud covered it, and the LORD's glory appeared.

⁴³ Moses and Aaron went to the front of the tent of meeting, ⁴⁴ and the LORD said to Moses, ⁴⁵ "Get away from this community so that I may consume them instantly." But they fell facedown.

⁴⁶ Then Moses told Aaron, "Take your firepan, place fire from the altar in it, and add incense. Go quickly to the community and make atonement for them, because wrath has come from the LORD; the plague has begun." ⁴⁷ So Aaron took his firepan as Moses had ordered, ran into the middle of the assembly, and saw that the plague had begun among the people. After he added incense, he made atonement for the people. ⁴⁸ He stood between the dead and the living, and the plague was halted. ⁴⁹ But those who died from the plague numbered 14,700, in addition to those who died because of the Korah incident. ⁵⁰ Aaron then returned to Moses at the entrance to the tent of meeting, since the plague had been halted.

⬥ GOING DEEPER

PSALM 46:8-11

⁸ Come, see the works of the LORD,
who brings devastation on the earth.

⁹ He makes wars cease throughout the earth.
He shatters bows and cuts spears to pieces;
he sets wagons ablaze.
¹⁰ "Stop fighting, and know that I am God,
exalted among the nations, exalted on the earth."
¹¹ The Lord of Armies is with us;
the God of Jacob is our stronghold.   *Selah*

MATTHEW 7:13-23

ENTERING THE KINGDOM

¹³ "Enter through the narrow gate. For the gate is wide and the road broad that leads to destruction, and there are many who go through it. ¹⁴ How narrow is the gate and difficult the road that leads to life, and few find it."

¹⁵ "Be on your guard against false prophets who come to you in sheep's clothing but inwardly are ravaging wolves. ¹⁶ You'll recognize them by their fruit. Are grapes gathered from thornbushes or figs from thistles? ¹⁷ In the same way, every good tree produces good fruit, but a bad tree produces bad fruit. ¹⁸ A good tree can't produce bad fruit; neither can a bad tree produce good fruit. ¹⁹ Every tree that doesn't produce good fruit is cut down and thrown into the fire. ²⁰ So you'll recognize them by their fruit."

²¹ "Not everyone who says to me, 'Lord, Lord,' will enter the kingdom of heaven, but only the one who does the will of my Father in heaven. ²² On that day many will say to me, 'Lord, Lord, didn't we prophesy in your name, drive out demons in your name, and do many miracles in your name?' ²³ Then I will announce to them, 'I never knew you. Depart from me, you lawbreakers!'"

NOTES

PROVISION FOR THE PRIESTHOOD

NUMBERS 17

AARON'S STAFF CHOSEN

¹ The LORD instructed Moses, ² "Speak to the Israelites and take one staff from them for each ancestral tribe, twelve staffs from all the leaders of their tribes. Write each man's name on his staff. ³ Write Aaron's name on Levi's staff, because there is to be one staff for the head of each tribe. ⁴ Then place them in the tent of meeting in front of the testimony where I meet with you. ⁵ The staff of the man I choose will sprout, and I will rid myself of the Israelites' complaints that they have been making about you."

⁶ So Moses spoke to the Israelites, and each of their leaders gave him a staff, one for each of the leaders of their tribes, twelve staffs in all. Aaron's staff was among them. ⁷ Moses placed the staffs before the LORD in the tent of the testimony.

⁸ The next day Moses entered the tent of the testimony and saw that Aaron's staff, representing the house of Levi, had sprouted, formed buds, blossomed, and produced almonds! ⁹ Moses then brought out all the staffs from the LORD's presence to all the Israelites. They saw them, and each man took his own staff. ¹⁰ The LORD told Moses, "Put Aaron's staff back in front of the testimony to be kept as a sign for the rebels, so that you may put an end to their complaints before me, or else they will die." ¹¹ So Moses did as the LORD commanded him.

¹² Then the Israelites declared to Moses, "Look, we're perishing! We're lost; we're all lost! ¹³ Anyone who comes near the LORD's tabernacle will die. Will we all perish?"

NUMBERS 18

PROVISION FOR THE PRIESTHOOD

¹ The LORD said to Aaron, "You, your sons, and your ancestral family will be responsible for iniquity against the sanctuary. You and your sons will be responsible for iniquity involving your priesthood. ² But also bring your relatives with you from the tribe of Levi, your ancestral tribe, so they may join you and assist you and your sons in front of the tent of the testimony.

³ They are to perform duties for you and for the whole tent. They must not come near the sanctuary equipment or the altar; otherwise, both they and you will die. ⁴ They are to join you and guard the tent of meeting, doing all the work at the tent, but no unauthorized person may come near you.

⁵ "You are to guard the sanctuary and the altar so that wrath may not fall on the Israelites again. ⁶ Look, I have selected your fellow Levites from the Israelites as a gift for you, assigned by the LORD to work at the tent of meeting. ⁷ But you and your sons will carry out your priestly responsibilities for everything concerning the altar and for what is inside the curtain, and you will do that work. I am giving you the work of the priesthood as a gift, but an unauthorized person who comes near the sanctuary will be put to death."

SUPPORT FOR THE PRIESTS AND LEVITES

⁸ Then the LORD spoke to Aaron, "Look, I have put you in charge of the contributions brought to me. As for all the holy offerings of the Israelites, I have given them to you and your sons as a portion and a permanent statute. ⁹ A portion of the holiest offerings kept from the fire will be yours; every one of their offerings that they give me, whether the grain offering, sin offering, or guilt offering will be most holy for you and your sons. ¹⁰ You are to eat it as a most holy offering. Every male may eat it; it is to be holy to you.

¹¹ "The contribution of their gifts also belongs to you. I have given all the Israelites' presentation offerings to you and to your sons and daughters as a permanent statute. Every ceremonially clean person in your house may eat it. ¹² I am giving you all the best of the fresh oil, new wine, and grain, which the Israelites give to the LORD as their firstfruits. ¹³ The firstfruits of all that is in their land, which they bring to the LORD, belong to you. Every clean person in your house may eat them.

¹⁴ "Everything in Israel that is permanently dedicated to the LORD belongs to you. ¹⁵ The firstborn of every living thing, human or animal, presented to the LORD belongs to you. But you must certainly redeem a human firstborn, and redeem the firstborn of an unclean animal. ¹⁶ You will pay the redemption price for a month-old male according to your assessment: five shekels of silver by the standard sanctuary shekel, which is twenty gerahs.

¹⁷ "However, you must not redeem the firstborn of an ox, a sheep, or a goat; they are holy. You are to splatter their blood on the altar and burn their fat as a food offering for a pleasing aroma to the LORD. ¹⁸ But their meat belongs to you. It belongs to you like the breast of the presentation offering and the right thigh.

¹⁹ "I give to you and to your sons and daughters all the holy contributions that the Israelites present to the LORD as a permanent statute. It is a permanent covenant of salt before the LORD for you as well as your offspring."

²⁰ The LORD told Aaron, "You will not have an inheritance in their land; there will be no portion among them for you. I am your portion and your inheritance among the Israelites.

²¹ "Look, I have given the Levites every tenth in Israel as an inheritance in return for the work they do, the work of the tent of meeting. ²² The Israelites must never again come near the tent of meeting, or they will incur guilt and

die. [23] The Levites will do the work of the tent of meeting, and they will bear the consequences of their iniquity. The Levites will not receive an inheritance among the Israelites; this is a permanent statute throughout your generations. [24] For I have given them the tenth that the Israelites present to the LORD as a contribution for their inheritance. That is why I told them that they would not receive an inheritance among the Israelites."

[25] The LORD instructed Moses, [26] "Speak to the Levites and tell them: When you receive from the Israelites the tenth that I have given you as your inheritance, you are to present part of it as an offering to the LORD—a tenth of the tenth. [27] Your offering will be credited to you as if it were your grain from the threshing floor or the full harvest from the winepress. [28] You are to present an offering to the LORD from every tenth you receive from the Israelites. Give some of it to the priest Aaron as an offering to the LORD. [29] You must present the entire offering due the LORD from all your gifts. The best part of the tenth is to be consecrated.

[30] "Tell them further: Once you have presented the best part of the tenth, and it is credited to you Levites as the produce of the threshing floor or the winepress, [31] then you and your household may eat it anywhere. It is your wage in return for your work at the tent of meeting. [32] You will not incur guilt because of it once you have presented the best part of it, but you must not defile the Israelites' holy offerings, so that you will not die."

♥ GOING DEEPER

LAMENTATIONS 3:24

I say, "The LORD is my portion,
therefore I will put my hope in him."

COLOSSIANS 3:23-24

[23] Whatever you do, do it from the heart, as something done for the Lord and not for people, [24] knowing that

YOU WILL RECEIVE THE REWARD OF AN INHERITANCE FROM THE LORD. YOU SERVE THE LORD CHRIST.

NOTES

GREAT IS THY FAITHFULNESS

WORDS:
THOMAS O. CHISHOLM

MUSIC:
WILLIAM M. RUNYAN

1. Great is Thy faith - ful - ness, O God, my Fa - ther; There is no
2. Sum - mer and win - ter, and spring - time and har - vest, Sun, moon and
3. Par - don for sin and a peace that en - dur - eth, Thine own dear

shad - ow of turn - ing with Thee. Thou chang - est not, Thy com -
stars in their cours - es a - bove join with all na - ture in
pres - ence to cheer and to guide; Strength for to - day and bright

pas - sions, they fail not; As Thou hast been, Thou for - ev - er wilt be.
man - i - fold wit - ness to Thy great faith - ful - ness, mer - cy and love.
hope for to - mor - row, Bless - ings all mine with ten thou - sand be - side!

WATER

DAY

FROM THE

19

ROCK

PURIFICATION RITUAL

1 The LORD spoke to Moses and Aaron, 2 "This is the legal statute that the LORD has commanded: Instruct the Israelites to bring you an unblemished red cow that has no defect and has never been yoked. 3 Give it to the priest Eleazar, and he will have it brought outside the camp and slaughtered in his presence. 4 The priest Eleazar is to take some of its blood with his finger and sprinkle it seven times toward the front of the tent of meeting. 5 The cow is to be burned in his sight. Its hide, flesh, and blood are to be burned along with its waste. 6 The priest is to take cedar wood, hyssop, and crimson yarn, and throw them onto the fire where the cow is burning. 7 Then the priest must wash his clothes and bathe his body in water; after that he may enter the camp, but he will remain ceremonially unclean until evening. 8 The one who burned the cow must also wash his clothes and bathe his body in water, and he will remain unclean until evening.

9 "A man who is clean is to gather up the cow's ashes and deposit them outside the camp in a ceremonially clean place. The ashes will be kept by the Israelite community for preparing the water to remove impurity; it is a sin offering. 10 Then the one who gathers up the cow's ashes must wash his clothes, and he will remain unclean until evening. This is a permanent statute for the Israelites and for the alien who resides among them.

11 "The person who touches any human corpse will be unclean for seven days. 12 He is to purify himself with the water on the third day and the seventh day; then he will be clean. But if he does not purify himself on the third and seventh days, he will not be clean. 13 Anyone who touches a body of a person who has died, and does not purify himself, defiles the tabernacle of the LORD. That person will be cut off from Israel. He remains unclean because the water for impurity has not been sprinkled on him, and his uncleanness is still on him.

14 "This is the law when a person dies in a tent: everyone who enters the tent and everyone who is already in the tent will be unclean for seven days, 15 and any open container without a lid tied on it is unclean. 16 Anyone in the open field who touches a person who has been killed by the sword or has died, or who even touches a human bone, or a grave, will be unclean for seven days. 17 For the purification of the unclean person, they are to take some of the ashes of the burnt sin offering, put them in a jar, and add fresh water to them. 18 A person who is clean is to take hyssop, dip it in the water, and sprinkle the tent, all the furnishings, and the people who were there. He is also to sprinkle the one who touched a bone, a grave, a corpse, or a person who had been killed.

19 "The one who is clean is to sprinkle the unclean person on the third day and the seventh day. After he purifies the unclean person on the seventh day, the one being purified must wash his clothes and bathe in water, and he will be clean by evening. 20 But a person who is unclean and does not purify himself, that person will be cut off from the assembly because he has defiled the sanctuary of the LORD. The water for impurity has not been sprinkled on him; he is unclean. 21 This is a permanent statute for them. The person who sprinkles the water for impurity is to wash his clothes, and whoever touches the water for impurity will be unclean

until evening. ²² Anything the unclean person touches will become unclean, and anyone who touches it will be unclean until evening."

NUMBERS 20:1-13

WATER FROM THE ROCK

¹ The entire Israelite community entered the Wilderness of Zin in the first month, and they settled in Kadesh. Miriam died and was buried there.

² There was no water for the community, so they assembled against Moses and Aaron. ³ The people quarreled with Moses and said, "If only we had perished when our brothers perished before the LORD. ⁴ Why have you brought the LORD's assembly into this wilderness for us and our livestock to die here? ⁵ Why have you led us up from Egypt to bring us to this evil place? It's not a place of grain, figs, vines, and pomegranates, and there is no water to drink!"

⁶ Then Moses and Aaron went from the presence of the assembly to the doorway of the tent of meeting. They fell facedown, and the glory of the LORD appeared to them. ⁷ The LORD spoke to Moses, ⁸ "Take the staff and assemble the community. You and your brother Aaron are to speak to the rock while they watch, and it will yield its water. You will bring out water for them from the rock and provide drink for the community and their livestock."

⁹ So Moses took the staff from the LORD's presence just as he had commanded him. ¹⁰ Moses and Aaron summoned the assembly in front of the rock, and Moses said to them, "Listen, you rebels! Must we bring water out of this rock for you?" ¹¹ Then Moses raised his hand and struck the rock twice with his

staff, so that abundant water gushed out, and the community and their livestock drank.

¹² But the Lᴏʀᴅ said to Moses and Aaron, "Because you did not trust me to demonstrate my holiness in the sight of the Israelites, you will not bring this assembly into the land I have given them." ¹³ These are the Waters of Meribah, where the Israelites quarreled with the Lᴏʀᴅ, and he demonstrated his holiness to them.

⬗ GOING DEEPER

PSALM 106:32-33

³² They angered the Lᴏʀᴅ at the Waters of Meribah,
and Moses suffered because of them,
³³ for they embittered his spirit,
and he spoke rashly with his lips.

JOHN 7:37-39

THE PROMISE OF THE SPIRIT

³⁷ On the last and most important day of the festival, Jesus stood up and cried out, "If anyone is thirsty, let him come to me and drink.

³⁸ THE ONE WHO BELIEVES IN ME, AS THE SCRIPTURE HAS SAID, WILL HAVE STREAMS OF LIVING WATER FLOW FROM DEEP WITHIN HIM."

³⁹ He said this about the Spirit. Those who believed in Jesus were going to receive the Spirit, for the Spirit had not yet been given because Jesus had not yet been glorified.

NOTES

WEEK 03 RESPONSE

OBSERVE

IN THIS WEEK'S READING, HOW DID YOU OBSERVE
GOD LEADING OR RESPONDING TO HIS PEOPLE?

HOW DID GOD'S PEOPLE RESPOND TO GOD OR HIS INSTRUCTION?

WHAT QUESTIONS DO YOU HAVE?

REFLECT

Where have you seen God's love, faithfulness, forgiveness, and/or justice around you this week?

LOVE	FAITHFULNESS

FORGIVENESS	JUSTICE

NUMBERS 14:18

THE LORD IS SLOW TO ANGER AND ABOUNDING IN FAITHFUL LOVE, FORGIVING INIQUITY AND REBELLION. BUT HE WILL NOT LEAVE THE GUILTY UNPUNISHED, BRINGING THE CONSEQUENCES OF THE FATHERS' INIQUITY ON THE CHILDREN TO THE THIRD AND FOURTH GENERATION.

© 2024 He Reads Truth. All rights reserved.

GRACE

Take this day to catch up on your reading,
pray, and rest in the presence of the Lord.

———

BUT AS THE ONE WHO CALLED
YOU IS HOLY, YOU ALSO ARE TO
BE HOLY IN ALL YOUR CONDUCT;
FOR IT IS WRITTEN, BE HOLY,
BECAUSE I AM HOLY.

1 PETER 1:15-16

DAY

WEEK

03

Scripture is God-breathed and true. When we memorize it,
we carry His Word with us wherever we go.

This week we will add the next section of Numbers 14:18,
a reminder of God's justice toward unrighteousness.

———

See tips for memorizing Scripture on page 180.

TRUTH

THE LORD IS SLOW TO ANGER AND ABOUNDING
IN FAITHFUL LOVE, FORGIVING INIQUITY AND
REBELLION. BUT HE WILL NOT LEAVE THE GUILTY
UNPUNISHED, BRINGING THE CONSEQUENCES OF
THE FATHERS' INIQUITY ON THE CHILDREN TO
THE THIRD AND FOURTH GENERATION.

NUMBERS 14:18

THE BRONZE SNAKE

———

SO MOSES MADE A BRONZE SNAKE AND MOUNTED IT ON A POLE. WHENEVER SOMEONE WAS BITTEN, AND HE LOOKED AT THE BRONZE SNAKE, HE RECOVERED.

NUMBERS 21:9

NUMBERS 20:14-29

EDOM DENIES PASSAGE

[14] Moses sent messengers from Kadesh to the king of **Edom**, "This is what your brother Israel says, 'You know all the hardships that have overtaken us. [15] Our ancestors went down to Egypt, and we lived in Egypt many years, but the Egyptians treated us and our ancestors badly. [16] When we cried out to the LORD, he heard our plea, and sent an angel, and brought us out of Egypt. Now look, we are in Kadesh, a city on the border of your territory. [17] Please let us travel through your land. We won't travel through any field or vineyard, or drink any well water. We will travel the King's Highway; we won't turn to the right or the left until we have traveled through your territory.'"

[18] But Edom answered him, "You will not travel through our land, or we will come out and confront you with the sword."

[19] "We will go on the main road," the Israelites replied to them, "and if we or our herds drink your water, we will pay its price. There will be no problem; only let us travel through on foot."

[20] Yet Edom insisted, "You may not travel through." And they came out to confront them with a large force of heavily-armed people. [21] Edom refused to allow Israel to travel through their territory, and Israel turned away from them.

AARON'S DEATH

[22] After they set out from Kadesh, the entire Israelite community came to Mount Hor. [23] The LORD said to Moses and Aaron at Mount Hor on the border of the land of Edom, [24] "Aaron will be gathered to his people; he will not enter the land I have given the Israelites, because you both rebelled against my command at the Waters of Meribah. [25] Take Aaron and his son Eleazar and bring them up Mount Hor.

ISRAEL'S WILDERNESS NEIGHBORS

EDOMITES

The descendants of Esau, the brother of Jacob, who occupied the region southeast of the promised land. Moses asked to pass through Edom, appealing to them as their "brother" (Nm 20:14), but their refusal forced Israel to travel around the land in their journey to the promised land.

26 Remove Aaron's garments and put them on his son Eleazar. Aaron will be gathered to his people and die there."

27 So Moses did as the LORD commanded, and they climbed Mount Hor in the sight of the whole community. 28 After Moses removed Aaron's garments and put them on his son Eleazar, Aaron died there on top of the mountain. Then Moses and Eleazar came down from the mountain. 29 When the whole community saw that Aaron had passed away, the entire house of Israel mourned for him thirty days.

NUMBERS 21:1-9

CANAANITE KING DEFEATED

1 When the Canaanite king of Arad, who lived in the Negev, heard that Israel was coming on the Atharim road, he fought against Israel and captured some prisoners. 2 Then Israel made a vow to the LORD, "If you will hand this people over to us, we will completely destroy their cities." 3 The LORD listened to Israel's request and handed the Canaanites over to them, and Israel completely destroyed them and their cities. So they named the place Hormah.

THE BRONZE SNAKE

4 Then they set out from Mount Hor by way of the Red Sea to bypass the land of Edom, but the people became impatient because of the journey. 5 The people spoke against God and Moses: "Why have you led us up from Egypt to die in the wilderness? There is no bread or water, and we detest this wretched food!" 6 Then the LORD sent poisonous snakes among the people, and they bit them so that many Israelites died.

7 The people then came to Moses and said, "We have sinned by speaking against the LORD and against you. Intercede with the LORD so that he will take the snakes away from us." And Moses interceded for the people.

8 Then the LORD said to Moses, "Make a snake image and mount it on a pole. When anyone who is bitten looks at it, he will recover." 9 So Moses made a bronze snake and mounted it on a pole. Whenever someone was bitten, and he looked at the bronze snake, he recovered.

GOING DEEPER

JOHN 3:14-17

14 "JUST AS MOSES LIFTED UP THE SNAKE IN THE WILDERNESS, SO THE SON OF MAN MUST BE LIFTED UP,

15 so that everyone who believes in him may have eternal life. 16 For God loved the world in this way: He gave his one and only Son, so that everyone who believes in him will not perish but have eternal life. 17 For God did not send his Son into the world to condemn the world, but to save the world through him."

NOTES

BALAK

SEEKS A

CURSE

JOURNEY AROUND MOAB

¹⁰ The Israelites set out and camped at Oboth. ¹¹ They set out from Oboth and camped at Iye-abarim in the wilderness that borders Moab on the east. ¹² From there they went and camped at Zered Valley. ¹³ They set out from there and camped on the other side of the Arnon River, in the wilderness that extends from the Amorite border, because the Arnon was the Moabite border between Moab and the Amorites. ¹⁴ Therefore it is stated in the Book of the LORD's Wars:

> Waheb in Suphah
> and the ravines of the Arnon,
> ¹⁵ even the slopes of the ravines
> that extend to the site of Ar
> and lie along the border of Moab.

¹⁶ From there they went to Beer, the well the LORD told Moses about, "Gather the people so I may give them water." ¹⁷ Then Israel sang this song:

> Spring up, well—sing to it!
> ¹⁸ The princes dug the well;
> the nobles of the people hollowed it out
> with a scepter and with their staffs.

They went from the wilderness to Mattanah, ¹⁹ from Mattanah to Nahaliel, from Nahaliel to Bamoth, ²⁰ from Bamoth to the valley in the territory of Moab near the Pisgah highlands that overlook the wasteland.

AMORITE KINGS DEFEATED

²¹ Israel sent messengers to say to King Sihon of the Amorites, ²² "Let us travel through your land. We won't go into the fields or vineyards. We won't drink any well water. We will travel the King's Highway until we have traveled through your territory." ²³ But Sihon would not let Israel travel through his territory. Instead, he gathered his whole army and went out to confront Israel in the wilderness. When he came to Jahaz, he fought against Israel. ²⁴ Israel struck him with the sword and took possession of his land from the Arnon to the Jabbok, but only up to the Ammonite border, because it was fortified.

²⁵ Israel took all the cities and lived in all these Amorite cities, including Heshbon and all its surrounding villages. ²⁶ Heshbon was the city of King Sihon of the Amorites, who had fought against the former king of Moab and had taken control of all his land as far as the Arnon. ²⁷ Therefore the poets say:

> Come to Heshbon, let it be rebuilt;
> let the city of Sihon be restored.
> ²⁸ For fire came out of Heshbon,
> a flame from the city of Sihon.
> It consumed Ar of Moab,
> the citizens of Arnon's heights.
> ²⁹ Woe to you, Moab!
> You have been destroyed, people of Chemosh!
> He gave up his sons as refugees,
> and his daughters into captivity
> to Sihon the Amorite king.
> ³⁰ We threw them down;
> Heshbon has been destroyed as far as Dibon.
> We caused desolation as far as Nophah,
> which reaches as far as Medeba.

³¹ So Israel lived in the Amorites' land. ³² After Moses sent spies to Jazer, Israel captured its surrounding villages and drove out the Amorites who were there.

ISRAEL'S WILDERNESS NEIGHBORS

MOABITES

The descendants of Lot, the nephew of Abraham, who occupied the eastern border of the promised land. The king of Moab summoned Balaam to curse Israel when he began to fear their size (Nm 22–24), but Balaam, at the Lord's intervention, blessed the nation instead. Still, after this encounter, Israel was led into idol worship by the Moabites (Nm 25).

[33] Then they turned and went up the road to Bashan, and King Og of Bashan came out against them with his whole army to do battle at Edrei. [34] But the LORD said to Moses, "Do not fear him, for I have handed him over to you along with his whole army and his land. Do to him as you did to King Sihon of the Amorites, who lived in Heshbon." [35] So they struck him, his sons, and his whole army until no one was left, and they took possession of his land.

NUMBERS 22

BALAK HIRES BALAAM

[1] The Israelites traveled on and camped in the plains of Moab near the Jordan across from Jericho. [2] Now Balak son of Zippor saw all that Israel had done to the Amorites. [3] Moab was terrified of the people because they were numerous, and Moab dreaded the Israelites. [4] So the **Moabites** said to the elders of Midian, "This horde will devour everything around us like an ox eats up the green plants in the field."

Since Balak son of Zippor was Moab's king at that time, [5] he sent messengers to Balaam son of Beor at Pethor, which is by the Euphrates in the land of his people. Balak said to him, "Look, a people has come out of Egypt; they cover the surface of the land and are living right across from me. [6] Please come and put a curse on these people for me because they are more powerful than I am. I may be able to defeat them and drive them out of the land, for I know that those you bless are blessed and those you curse are cursed."

[7] The elders of Moab and Midian departed with fees for divination in hand. They came to Balaam and reported Balak's words to him. [8] He said to them, "Spend the night here, and I will give you the answer the LORD tells me." So the officials of Moab stayed with Balaam.

⁹ Then God came to Balaam and asked, "Who are these men with you?"

¹⁰ Balaam replied to God, "Balak son of Zippor, king of Moab, sent this message to me: ¹¹ 'Look, a people has come out of Egypt, and they cover the surface of the land. Now come and put a curse on them for me. I may be able to fight against them and drive them away.'"

¹² Then God said to Balaam, "You are not to go with them. You are not to curse this people, for they are blessed."

¹³ So Balaam got up the next morning and said to Balak's officials, "Go back to your land, because the LORD has refused to let me go with you."

¹⁴ The officials of Moab arose, returned to Balak, and reported, "Balaam refused to come with us."

¹⁵ Balak sent officials again who were more numerous and higher in rank than the others. ¹⁶ They came to Balaam and said to him, "This is what Balak son of Zippor says: 'Let nothing keep you from coming to me, ¹⁷ for I will greatly honor you and do whatever you ask me. So please come and put a curse on these people for me!'"

¹⁸ But Balaam responded to the servants of Balak, "If Balak were to give me his house full of silver and gold, I could not go against the command of the LORD my God to do anything small or great. ¹⁹ Please stay here overnight as the others did, so that I may find out what else the LORD has to tell me."

²⁰ God came to Balaam at night and said to him, "Since these men have come to summon you, get up and go with them, but you must only do what I tell you." ²¹ When he got up in the morning, Balaam saddled his donkey and went with the officials of Moab.

²² But God was incensed that Balaam was going, and the angel of the LORD took his stand on the path to oppose him. Balaam was riding his donkey, and his two servants were with him. ²³ When the donkey saw the angel of the LORD standing on the path with a drawn sword in his hand, she turned off the path and went into the field. So Balaam hit her to return her to the path. ²⁴ Then the angel of the LORD stood in a narrow passage between the vineyards, with a stone wall on either side. ²⁵ The donkey saw the angel of the LORD and pressed herself against the wall, squeezing Balaam's foot against it. So he hit her once again. ²⁶ The angel of the LORD went ahead and stood in a narrow place where there was no room to turn to the right or the left. ²⁷ When the donkey saw the angel of the LORD, she crouched down under Balaam. So he became furious and beat the donkey with his stick.

²⁸ Then the LORD opened the donkey's mouth, and she asked Balaam, "What have I done to you that you have beaten me these three times?"

²⁹ Balaam answered the donkey, "You made me look like a fool. If I had a sword in my hand, I'd kill you now!"

³⁰ But the donkey said, "Am I not the donkey you've ridden all your life until today? Have I ever treated you this way before?"

"No," he replied.

³¹ Then the LORD opened Balaam's eyes, and he saw the angel of the LORD standing in the path with a drawn sword in his hand. Balaam knelt low and bowed in worship on his face. ³² The angel of the LORD asked him, "Why have you beaten your donkey these three times? Look, I came out to oppose you, because I consider what you are doing to be evil. ³³ The donkey saw me and turned away from me these three times. If she had not turned away from me, I would have killed you by now and let her live."

³⁴ Balaam said to the angel of the LORD, "I have sinned, for I did not know that you were standing in the path to confront me. And now, if it is evil in your sight, I will go back."

³⁵ Then the angel of the LORD said to Balaam, "Go with the men, but you are to say only what I tell you." So Balaam went with Balak's officials.

³⁶ When Balak heard that Balaam was coming, he went out to meet him at the Moabite city on the Arnon border at the edge of his territory. ³⁷ Balak asked Balaam, "Did I not send you an urgent summons? Why didn't you come to me? Am I really not able to reward you?"

³⁸ Balaam said to him, "Look, I have come to you, but can I say anything I want? I must speak only the message God puts in my mouth." ³⁹ So Balaam went with Balak, and they came to Kiriath-huzoth. ⁴⁰ Balak sacrificed cattle, sheep,

and goats and sent for Balaam and the officials who were with him.

⁴¹ In the morning, Balak took Balaam and brought him to Bamoth-baal. From there he saw the outskirts of the people's camp.

🦅 GOING DEEPER

PSALM 37:1-3

INSTRUCTION IN WISDOM

Of David.

¹ Do not be agitated by evildoers;
do not envy those who do wrong.
² For they wither quickly like grass
and wilt like tender green plants.

³ Trust in the LORD and do what is good;
dwell in the land and live securely.

2 PETER 2:14-16

¹⁴ They have eyes full of adultery that never stop looking for sin. They seduce unstable people and have hearts trained in greed. Children under a curse! ¹⁵ They have gone astray by abandoning the straight path and have followed the path of Balaam, the son of Bosor, who loved the wages of wickedness ¹⁶ but received a rebuke for his lawlessness: A speechless donkey spoke with a human voice and restrained the prophet's madness.

BALAAM'S ORACLES

NUMBERS 23

BALAAM'S ORACLES

¹ Then Balaam said to Balak, "Build me seven altars here and prepare seven bulls and seven rams for me." ² So Balak did as Balaam directed, and they offered a bull and a ram on each altar. ³ Balaam said to Balak, "Stay here by your burnt offering while I am gone. Maybe the LORD will meet with me. I will tell you whatever he reveals to me." So he went to a barren hill.

⁴ God met with him and Balaam said to him, "I have arranged seven altars and offered a bull and a ram on each altar." ⁵ Then the LORD put a message in Balaam's mouth and said, "Return to Balak and say what I tell you."

⁶ So he returned to Balak, who was standing there by his burnt offering with all the officials of Moab.

BALAAM'S FIRST ORACLE

⁷ Balaam proclaimed his poem:

Balak brought me from Aram;
the king of Moab, from the
    eastern mountains:
"Come, put a curse on Jacob for me;

come, denounce Israel!"
⁸ How can I curse someone God
    has not cursed?
How can I denounce someone the
    LORD has not denounced?
⁹ I see them from the top of rocky cliffs,
and I watch them from the hills.
There is a people living alone;
it does not consider itself among the nations.
¹⁰ Who has counted the dust of Jacob
or numbered even one-fourth of Israel?
Let me die the death of the upright;
let the end of my life be like theirs.

¹¹ "What have you done to me?" Balak asked Balaam. "I brought you to curse my enemies, but look, you have only blessed them!"

¹² He answered, "Shouldn't I say exactly what the LORD puts in my mouth?"

BALAAM'S SECOND ORACLE

¹³ Then Balak said to him, "Please come with me to another place where you can see them. You will only see the outskirts of their camp; you won't see all of them. From there, put a

_____

_____

_____

_____

_____

_____

_____

_____

_____

_____

_____

_____

_____

_____

_____

_____

_____

_____

_____

_____

_____

_____

_____

curse on them for me." [14] So Balak took him to Lookout Field on top of Pisgah, built seven altars, and offered a bull and a ram on each altar.

[15] Balaam said to Balak, "Stay here by your burnt offering while I seek the LORD over there."

[16] The LORD met with Balaam and put a message in his mouth. Then he said, "Return to Balak and say what I tell you."

[17] So he returned to Balak, who was standing there by his burnt offering with the officials of Moab. Balak asked him, "What did the LORD say?"

[18] Balaam proclaimed his poem:

Balak, get up and listen;
son of Zippor, pay attention to what I say!
[19] God is not a man, that he might lie,
or a son of man, that he might change his mind.
Does he speak and not act,
or promise and not fulfill?
[20] I have indeed received a command to bless;
since he has blessed, I cannot change it.
[21] He considers no disaster for Jacob;
he sees no trouble for Israel.
The LORD their God is with them,
and there is rejoicing over the King among them.
[22] God brought them out of Egypt;
he is like the horns of a wild ox for them.
[23] There is no magic curse against Jacob
and no divination against Israel.
It will now be said about Jacob and Israel,
"What great things God has done!"
[24] A people rise up like a lioness;
they rouse themselves like a lion.
They will not lie down until they devour the prey
and drink the blood of the slain.

[25] Then Balak told Balaam, "Don't curse them and don't bless them!"

26 But Balaam answered him, "Didn't I tell you: Whatever the Lord says, I must do?"

BALAAM'S THIRD ORACLE

27 Again Balak said to Balaam, "Please come. I will take you to another place. Maybe it will be agreeable to God that you can put a curse on them for me there." 28 So Balak took Balaam to the top of Peor, which overlooks the wasteland.

29 Balaam told Balak, "Build me seven altars here and prepare seven bulls and seven rams for me." 30 So Balak did as Balaam said and offered a bull and a ram on each altar.

NUMBERS 24

1 Since Balaam saw that it pleased the Lord to bless Israel, he did not go to seek omens as on previous occasions, but turned toward the wilderness. 2 When Balaam looked up and saw Israel encamped tribe by tribe, the Spirit of God came on him, 3 and he proclaimed his poem:

The oracle of Balaam son of Beor,
the oracle of the man whose eyes are opened,
4 the oracle of one who hears the sayings of God,
who sees a vision from the Almighty,
who falls into a trance with his eyes uncovered:
5 How beautiful are your tents, Jacob,
your dwellings, Israel.
6 They stretch out like river valleys,
like gardens beside a stream,
like aloes the Lord has planted,
like cedars beside the water.
7 Water will flow from his buckets,
and his seed will be by abundant water.
His king will be greater than Agag,
and his kingdom will be exalted.
8 God brought him out of Egypt;
he is like the horns of a wild ox for them.
He will feed on enemy nations

and gnaw their bones;
he will strike them with his arrows.
⁹ He crouches, he lies down like a lion
or a lioness—who dares to rouse him?
Those who bless you will be blessed,
and those who curse you will be cursed.

¹⁰ Then Balak became furious with Balaam, struck his hands together, and said to him, "I summoned you to put a curse on my enemies, but instead, you have blessed them these three times. ¹¹ Now go to your home! I said I would reward you richly, but look, the LORD has denied you a reward."

¹² Balaam answered Balak, "Didn't I previously tell the messengers you sent me: ¹³ If Balak were to give me his house full of silver and gold, I could not go against the LORD's command, to do anything good or bad of my own will? I will say whatever the LORD says. ¹⁴ Now I am going back to my people, but first, let me warn you what these people will do to your people in the future."

BALAAM'S FOURTH ORACLE

¹⁵ Then he proclaimed his poem:

The oracle of Balaam son of Beor,
the oracle of the man whose eyes are opened;

¹⁶ the oracle of one who hears the sayings
of God
and has knowledge from the Most High,
who sees a vision from the Almighty,
who falls into a trance with his
eyes uncovered:
¹⁷ I see him, but not now;
I perceive him, but not near.
A star will come from Jacob,
and a scepter will arise from Israel.
He will smash the forehead of Moab
and strike down all the Shethites.
¹⁸ Edom will become a possession;
Seir will become a possession of its enemies,
but Israel will be triumphant.
¹⁹ One who comes from Jacob will rule;
he will destroy the city's survivors.

²⁰ Then Balaam saw Amalek and proclaimed his poem:

Amalek was first among the nations,
but his future is destruction.

²¹ Next he saw the Kenites and proclaimed his poem:

Your dwelling place is enduring;
your nest is set in the cliffs.
²² Kain will be destroyed
when Asshur takes you captive.

²³ Once more he proclaimed his poem:

> Ah, who can live when God does this?
> ²⁴ Ships will come from the coast of Kittim;
> they will carry out raids against Asshur
>   and Eber,
> but they too will come to destruction.

²⁵ Balaam then arose and went back to his homeland, and Balak also went his way.

💙 GOING DEEPER

GENESIS 12:2-3

² "I will make you into a great nation,
I will bless you,
I will make your name great,
and you will be a blessing.
³ I will bless those who bless you,
I will curse anyone who treats you
    with contempt,
and all the peoples on earth
will be blessed through you."

ROMANS 8:31

WHAT, THEN, ARE WE TO SAY ABOUT THESE THINGS? IF GOD IS FOR US, WHO IS AGAINST US?

ISRAEL

DAY

WORSHIPS

25

BAAL

ISRAEL WORSHIPS BAAL

¹ While Israel was staying in the Acacia Grove, the people began to prostitute themselves with the women of Moab. ² The women invited them to the sacrifices for their gods, and the people ate and bowed in worship to their gods. ³ So Israel aligned itself with Baal of Peor, and the LORD's anger burned against Israel. ⁴ The LORD said to Moses, "Take all the leaders of the people and execute them in broad daylight before the LORD so that his burning anger may turn away from Israel."

⁵ So Moses told Israel's judges, "Kill each of the men who aligned themselves with Baal of Peor."

PHINEHAS INTERVENES

⁶ An Israelite man came bringing a Midianite woman to his relatives in the sight of Moses and the whole Israelite community while they were weeping at the entrance to the tent of meeting. ⁷ When Phinehas son of Eleazar, son of Aaron the priest, saw this, he got up from the assembly, took a spear in his hand, ⁸ followed the Israelite man into the tent, and drove it through both the Israelite man and the woman—through her belly. Then the plague on the Israelites was stopped, ⁹ but those who died in the plague numbered twenty-four thousand.

¹⁰ The LORD spoke to Moses, ¹¹ "Phinehas son of Eleazar, son of Aaron the priest, has turned back my wrath from the Israelites because he was zealous among them with my zeal, so that I did not destroy the Israelites in my zeal. ¹² Therefore declare: I grant him my covenant of peace. ¹³ It will be a covenant of perpetual priesthood for him and his future descendants, because he was zealous for his God and made atonement for the Israelites."

¹⁴ The name of the slain Israelite man, who was struck dead with the Midianite woman, was Zimri son of

ISRAEL'S WILDERNESS NEIGHBORS

MIDIANITES
The descendants of Midian, Abraham's son by Keturah, who occupied the land east of Sinai. They formed a treaty with Moab to hire Balaam and warred with the Israelites (Nm 31).

Salu, the leader of a Simeonite family. [15] The name of the slain Midianite woman was Cozbi, the daughter of Zur, a tribal head of a family in Midian.

VENGEANCE AGAINST THE MIDIANITES

[16] The LORD told Moses, [17] "Attack the **Midianites** and strike them dead. [18] For they attacked you with the treachery that they used against you in the Peor incident. They did the same in the case involving their sister Cozbi, daughter of the Midianite leader who was killed the day the plague came at Peor."

♥ GOING DEEPER

EXODUS 34:10-16

COVENANT OBLIGATIONS

[10] And the LORD responded, "Look, I am making a covenant. In the presence of all your people I will perform wonders that have never been done in the whole earth or in any nation. All the people you live among will see the LORD's work, for what I am doing with you is awe-inspiring. [11] Observe what I command you today. I am going to drive out before you the Amorites, Canaanites, Hethites, Perizzites, Hivites, and Jebusites. [12] Be careful not to make a treaty with the inhabitants of the land that you are going to enter; otherwise, they will become a snare among you. [13] Instead, you must tear down their altars, smash their sacred pillars, and chop down their Asherah poles. [14] Because the LORD is jealous for his reputation, you are never to bow down to another god. He is a jealous God.

[15] "Do not make a treaty with the inhabitants of the land, or else when they prostitute themselves with their gods and sacrifice to their gods, they will invite you, and you will eat their sacrifices. [16] Then you will take some of their daughters as brides for your sons.

Their daughters will prostitute themselves with their gods and cause your sons to prostitute themselves with their gods."

PSALM 16:4

THE SORROWS OF THOSE WHO
TAKE ANOTHER GOD
FOR THEMSELVES WILL MULTIPLY;

I will not pour out their drink offerings of blood, and I will not speak their names with my lips.

ROMANS 1:25

They exchanged the truth of God for a lie, and worshiped and served what has been created instead of the Creator, who is praised forever. Amen.

1 CORINTHIANS 10:14-22

WARNING AGAINST IDOLATRY

[14] So then, my dear friends, flee from idolatry. [15] I am speaking as to sensible people. Judge for yourselves what I am saying. [16] The cup of blessing that we bless, is it not a sharing in the blood of Christ? The bread that we break, is it not a sharing in the body of Christ? [17] Because there is one bread, we who are many are one body, since all of us share the one bread. [18] Consider the people of Israel. Do not those who eat the sacrifices participate in the altar? [19] What am I saying then? That food sacrificed to idols is anything, or that an idol is anything? [20] No, but I do say that what they sacrifice, they sacrifice to demons and not to God. I do not want you to be participants with demons! [21] You cannot drink the cup of the Lord and the cup of demons. You cannot share in the Lord's table and the table of demons. [22] Or are we provoking the Lord to jealousy? Are we stronger than he?

NUMBERS 26

THE SECOND CENSUS

¹ After the plague, the Lord said to Moses and Eleazar son of Aaron the priest, ² "Take a census of the entire Israelite community by their ancestral families of those twenty years old or more who can serve in Israel's army."

³ So Moses and the priest Eleazar said to them in the plains of Moab by the Jordan across from Jericho, ⁴ "Take a census of those twenty years old or more, as the Lord had commanded Moses and the Israelites who came out of the land of Egypt."

⁵ Reuben was the firstborn of Israel.
Reuben's descendants:
the Hanochite clan from Hanoch;
the Palluite clan from Pallu;
⁶ the Hezronite clan from Hezron;
the Carmite clan from Carmi.
⁷ These were the Reubenite clans,
and their registered men numbered 43,730.
⁸ The son of Pallu was Eliab.
⁹ The sons of Eliab were Nemuel, Dathan, and Abiram.

(It was Dathan and Abiram, chosen by the community, who fought against Moses and Aaron; they and Korah's followers fought against the Lord. ¹⁰ The earth opened its mouth and swallowed them with Korah, when his followers died and the fire consumed 250 men. They serve as a warning sign. ¹¹ The sons of Korah, however, did not die.)

¹² Simeon's descendants by their clans:
the Nemuelite clan from Nemuel;
the Jaminite clan from Jamin;
the Jachinite clan from Jachin;
¹³ the Zerahite clan from Zerah;
the Shaulite clan from Shaul.
¹⁴ These were the Simeonite clans, numbering 22,200 men.
¹⁵ Gad's descendants by their clans:
the Zephonite clan from Zephon;
the Haggite clan from Haggi;
the Shunite clan from Shuni;

¹⁶ the Oznite clan from Ozni;
the Erite clan from Eri;
¹⁷ the Arodite clan from Arod;
the Arelite clan from Areli.
¹⁸ These were the Gadite clans numbered by their registered men: 40,500.

¹⁹ Judah's sons included Er and Onan, but they died in the land of Canaan. ²⁰ Judah's descendants by their clans:

the Shelanite clan from Shelah;
the Perezite clan from Perez;
the Zerahite clan from Zerah.
²¹ The descendants of Perez:
the Hezronite clan from Hezron;
the Hamulite clan from Hamul.
²² These were Judah's clans numbered by their registered men: 76,500.
²³ Issachar's descendants by their clans:
the Tolaite clan from Tola;
the Punite clan from Puvah;
²⁴ the Jashubite clan from Jashub;
the Shimronite clan from Shimron.
²⁵ These were Issachar's clans numbered by their registered men: 64,300.
²⁶ Zebulun's descendants by their clans:
the Seredite clan from Sered;
the Elonite clan from Elon;
the Jahleelite clan from Jahleel.
²⁷ These were the Zebulunite clans numbered by their registered men: 60,500.
²⁸ Joseph's descendants by their clans from Manasseh and Ephraim:
²⁹ Manasseh's descendants:
the Machirite clan from Machir.
Machir fathered Gilead;
the Gileadite clan from Gilead.
³⁰ These were Gilead's descendants:
the Iezerite clan from Iezer;
the Helekite clan from Helek;
³¹ the Asrielite clan from Asriel;

the Shechemite clan from Shechem;
³² the Shemidaite clan from Shemida;
the Hepherite clan from Hepher;

³³ Zelophehad son of Hepher had no sons—only daughters. The names of Zelophehad's daughters were Mahlah, Noah, Hoglah, Milcah, and Tirzah.

³⁴ These were Manasseh's clans, numbered by their registered men: 52,700.
³⁵ These were Ephraim's descendants by their clans:
the Shuthelahite clan from Shuthelah;
the Becherite clan from Becher;
the Tahanite clan from Tahan.
³⁶ These were Shuthelah's descendants:
the Eranite clan from Eran.
³⁷ These were the Ephraimite clans numbered by their registered men: 32,500.
These were Joseph's descendants by their clans.
³⁸ Benjamin's descendants by their clans:
the Belaite clan from Bela;
the Ashbelite clan from Ashbel;
the Ahiramite clan from Ahiram;
³⁹ the Shuphamite clan from Shupham;
the Huphamite clan from Hupham.
⁴⁰ Bela's descendants from Ard and Naaman:
the Ardite clan from Ard;
the Naamite clan from Naaman.
⁴¹ These were the Benjaminite clans numbered by their registered men: 45,600.
⁴² These were Dan's descendants by their clans:
the Shuhamite clan from Shuham.
These were the clans of Dan by their clans.
⁴³ All the Shuhamite clans numbered by their registered men: 64,400.
⁴⁴ Asher's descendants by their clans:
the Imnite clan from Imnah;
the Ishvite clan from Ishvi;
the Beriite clan from Beriah.
⁴⁵ From Beriah's descendants:

_____

_____

_____

_____

_____

_____

_____

_____

_____

_____

_____

_____

_____

_____

_____

_____

_____

_____

_____

_____

_____

_____

_____

_____

_____

the Heberite clan from Heber;

the Malchielite clan from Malchiel.

[46] And the name of Asher's daughter was Serah.

[47] These were the Asherite clans numbered by their registered men: 53,400.

[48] Naphtali's descendants by their clans:

the Jahzeelite clan from Jahzeel;

the Gunite clan from Guni;

[49] the Jezerite clan from Jezer;

the Shillemite clan from Shillem.

[50] These were the Naphtali clans numbered by their registered men: 45,400.

[51] These registered Israelite men numbered 601,730.

[52] The Lord spoke to Moses, [53] "The land is to be divided among them as an inheritance based on the number of names. [54] Increase the inheritance for a large tribe and decrease it for a small one. Each is to be given its inheritance according to those who were registered in it. [55] The land is to be divided by lot; they will receive an inheritance according to the names of their ancestral tribes. [56] Each inheritance will be divided by lot among the larger and smaller tribes."

[57] These were the Levites registered by their clans:

the Gershonite clan from Gershon;

the Kohathite clan from Kohath;

the Merarite clan from Merari.

[58] These were the Levite family groups:

the Libnite clan,

the Hebronite clan,

the Mahlite clan,

the Mushite clan,

and the Korahite clan.

Kohath was the ancestor of Amram. [59] The name of Amram's wife was Jochebed, a descendant of Levi, born to Levi in Egypt. She bore to Amram: Aaron, Moses, and their sister Miriam. [60] Nadab, Abihu, Eleazar, and Ithamar were born to Aaron, [61] but Nadab and Abihu died when they presented unauthorized fire before the LORD. [62] Those registered were 23,000, every male one month old or more; they were not registered among the other Israelites, because no inheritance was given to them among the Israelites.

[63] These were the ones registered by Moses and the priest Eleazar when they registered the Israelites on the plains of Moab by the Jordan across from Jericho. [64] But among them there was not one of those who had been registered by Moses and the priest Aaron when they registered the Israelites in the Wilderness of Sinai. [65] For the LORD had said to them that they would all die in the wilderness. None of them was left except Caleb son of Jephunneh and Joshua son of Nun.

◥ GOING DEEPER

DEUTERONOMY 2:14-15

[14] The time we spent traveling from Kadesh-barnea until we crossed the Zered Valley was thirty-eight years until the entire generation of fighting men had perished from the camp, as the LORD had sworn to them. [15] Indeed, the LORD's hand was against them, to eliminate them from the camp until they had all perished.

PSALM 95:10-11

[10] For forty years I was disgusted with that generation;
I said, "They are a people whose hearts go astray;
they do not know my ways."
[11] So I swore in my anger,
"They will not enter my rest."

WEEK 04 RESPONSE

OBSERVE

IN THIS WEEK'S READING, HOW DID YOU OBSERVE
GOD LEADING OR RESPONDING TO HIS PEOPLE?

HOW DID GOD'S PEOPLE RESPOND TO GOD OR HIS INSTRUCTION?

WHAT QUESTIONS DO YOU HAVE?

REFLECT

Where have you seen God's love, faithfulness, forgiveness, and/or justice around you this week?

LOVE	FAITHFULNESS

FORGIVENESS	JUSTICE

NUMBERS 14:18

THE LORD IS SLOW TO ANGER AND ABOUNDING IN FAITHFUL LOVE, FORGIVING INIQUITY AND REBELLION. BUT HE WILL NOT LEAVE THE GUILTY UNPUNISHED, BRINGING THE CONSEQUENCES OF THE FATHERS' INIQUITY ON THE CHILDREN TO THE THIRD AND FOURTH GENERATION.

© 2024 He Reads Truth. All rights reserved.

GRACE

Take this day to catch up on your reading,
pray, and rest in the presence of the Lord.

———

WHAT, THEN, ARE WE TO SAY
ABOUT THESE THINGS? IF GOD IS
FOR US, WHO IS AGAINST US?

ROMANS 8:31

DAY

WEEK
03

WEEKLY

Scripture is God-breathed and true. When we memorize it,
we carry His Word with us wherever we go.

This week we will commit to memory the final portion
of Numbers 14:18, a stark reminder of the lasting effects
of sin.

———

See tips for memorizing Scripture on page 180.

TRUTH

THE LORD IS SLOW TO ANGER AND ABOUNDING
IN FAITHFUL LOVE, FORGIVING INIQUITY AND
REBELLION. BUT HE WILL NOT LEAVE THE GUILTY
UNPUNISHED, <u>BRINGING THE CONSEQUENCES OF
THE FATHERS' INIQUITY ON THE CHILDREN TO
THE THIRD AND FOURTH GENERATION.</u>

NUMBERS 14:18

WEEK
04

JOSHUA COMMISSIONED TO SUCCEED MOSES

NUMBERS 27

A CASE OF DAUGHTERS' INHERITANCE

[1] The daughters of Zelophehad approached; Zelophehad was the son of Hepher, son of Gilead, son of Machir, son of Manasseh from the clans of Manasseh, the son of Joseph. These were the names of his daughters: Mahlah, Noah, Hoglah, Milcah, and Tirzah. [2] They stood before Moses, the priest Eleazar, the leaders, and the entire community at the entrance to the tent of meeting and said, [3] "Our father died in the wilderness, but he was not among Korah's followers, who gathered together against the LORD. Instead, he died because of his own sin, and he had no sons. [4] Why should the name of our father be taken away from his clan? Since he had no son, give us property among our father's brothers."

[5] Moses brought their case before the LORD, [6] and the LORD answered him, [7] "What Zelophehad's daughters say is correct. You are to give them hereditary property among their father's brothers and transfer their father's inheritance to them. [8] Tell the Israelites: When a man dies without having a son, transfer his inheritance to his daughter. [9] If he has no daughter, give his inheritance to his brothers. [10] If he has no brothers, give his inheritance to his father's brothers. [11] If his father has no brothers, give his inheritance to the nearest relative of his clan, and he will take possession of it. This is to be a statutory ordinance for the Israelites as the LORD commanded Moses."

JOSHUA COMMISSIONED TO SUCCEED MOSES

[12] Then the LORD said to Moses, "Go up this mountain of the Abarim range and see the land that I have given the Israelites. [13] After you have

seen it, you will also be gathered to your people, as Aaron your brother was. ¹⁴ When the community quarreled in the Wilderness of Zin, both of you rebelled against my command to demonstrate my holiness in their sight at the waters." Those were the Waters of Meribah-kadesh in the Wilderness of Zin.

¹⁵ So Moses appealed to the Lord, ¹⁶ "May the Lord, the God who gives breath to all, appoint a man over the community ¹⁷ who will go out before them and come back in before them, and who will bring them out and bring them in, so that the Lord's community won't be like sheep without a shepherd."

¹⁸ The Lord replied to Moses, "Take Joshua son of Nun, a man who has the Spirit in him, and lay your hands on him. ¹⁹ Have him stand before the priest Eleazar and the whole community, and commission him in their sight. ²⁰ Confer some of your authority on him so that the entire Israelite community will obey him. ²¹ He will stand before the priest Eleazar who will consult the Lord for him with the decision of the Urim. He and all the Israelites with him, even the entire community, will go out and come back in at his command."

²² Moses did as the Lord commanded him. He took Joshua, had him stand before the priest Eleazar and the entire community, ²³ laid his hands on him, and commissioned him, as the Lord had spoken through Moses.

♥ GOING DEEPER

JOSHUA 1:1-9

ENCOURAGEMENT OF JOSHUA

¹ After the death of Moses the Lord's servant, the Lord spoke to Joshua son of Nun, Moses's assistant: ² "Moses my servant is dead. Now you and all the people prepare to cross over the Jordan to the land I

am giving the Israelites. ³ I have given you every place where the sole of your foot treads, just as I promised Moses. ⁴ Your territory will be from the wilderness and Lebanon to the great river, the Euphrates River—all the land of the Hittites—and west to the Mediterranean Sea. ⁵ No one will be able to stand against you as long as you live.

I WILL BE WITH YOU, JUST AS I WAS WITH MOSES.

I will not leave you or abandon you.

⁶ "Be strong and courageous, for you will distribute the land I swore to their ancestors to give them as an inheritance. ⁷ Above all, be strong and very courageous to observe carefully the whole instruction my servant Moses commanded you. Do not turn from it to the right or the left, so that you will have success wherever you go. ⁸ This book of instruction must not depart from your mouth; you are to meditate on it day and night so that you may carefully observe everything written in it. For then you will prosper and succeed in whatever you do. ⁹ Haven't I commanded you: be strong and courageous? Do not be afraid or discouraged, for the LORD your God is with you wherever you go."

HEBREWS 11:13-16

¹³ These all died in faith, although they had not received the things that were promised. But they saw them from a distance, greeted them, and confessed that they were foreigners and temporary residents on the earth. ¹⁴ Now those who say such things make it clear that they are seeking a homeland. ¹⁵ If they were thinking about where they came from, they would have had an opportunity to return. ¹⁶ But they now desire a better place—a heavenly one. Therefore, God is not ashamed to be called their God, for he has prepared a city for them.

NOTES

OFFERINGS, FESTIVALS, AND LAWS

NUMBERS 28

PRESCRIBED OFFERINGS

[1] The LORD spoke to Moses, [2] "Command the Israelites and say to them: Be sure to present to me at its appointed time my offering and my food as my food offering, a pleasing aroma to me. [3] And say to them: This is the food offering you are to present to the LORD:

DAILY OFFERINGS

"Each day present two unblemished year-old male lambs as a regular burnt offering. [4] Offer one lamb in the morning and the other lamb at twilight, [5] along with two quarts of fine flour for a grain offering mixed with a quart of olive oil from crushed olives. [6] It is a regular burnt offering established at Mount Sinai for a pleasing aroma, a food offering to the LORD. [7] The drink offering is to be a quart with each lamb. Pour out the offering of beer to the LORD in the sanctuary area. [8] Offer the second lamb at twilight, along with the same kind of grain offering and drink offering as in the morning. It is a food offering, a pleasing aroma to the LORD.

SABBATH OFFERINGS

[9] "On the Sabbath day present two unblemished year-old male lambs, four quarts of fine flour mixed with oil as a grain offering, and its drink offering. [10] It is the burnt offering for every Sabbath, in addition to the regular burnt offering and its drink offering.

MONTHLY OFFERINGS

[11] "At the beginning of each of your months present a burnt offering to the LORD: two young bulls, one ram, seven male lambs a year old—all unblemished— [12] with six quarts of fine flour mixed with oil as a grain offering for each bull, four quarts of fine flour mixed with oil as a grain offering for the ram, [13] and two quarts of fine flour mixed with oil as a grain offering for each lamb. It is a burnt offering, a pleasing aroma, a food offering to the LORD. [14] Their drink offerings are to be two quarts of wine with each bull, one and a third quarts with the ram, and one quart with each male lamb.

This is the monthly burnt offering for all the months of the year. ¹⁵ And one male goat is to be offered as a sin offering to the LORD, in addition to the regular burnt offering with its drink offering.

¹⁶ "The Passover to the LORD comes in the first month, on the fourteenth day of the month. ¹⁷ On the fifteenth day of this month there will be a festival; unleavened bread is to be eaten for seven days. ¹⁸ On the first day there is to be a sacred assembly; you are not to do any daily work. ¹⁹ Present a food offering, a burnt offering to the LORD: two young bulls, one ram, and seven male lambs a year old. Your animals are to be unblemished. ²⁰ The grain offering with them is to be of fine flour mixed with oil; offer six quarts with each bull and four quarts with the ram. ²¹ Offer two quarts with each of the seven lambs ²² and one male goat for a sin offering to make atonement for yourselves. ²³ Offer these with the morning burnt offering that is part of the regular burnt offering. ²⁴ You are to offer the same food each day for seven days as a food offering, a pleasing aroma to the LORD. It is to be offered with its drink offering and the regular burnt offering. ²⁵ On the seventh day you are to hold a sacred assembly; you are not to do any daily work.

OFFERINGS FOR THE FESTIVAL OF WEEKS

²⁶ "On the day of firstfruits, you are to hold a sacred assembly when you present an offering of new grain to the LORD at your Festival of Weeks; you are not to do any daily work. ²⁷ Present a burnt offering as a pleasing aroma to the LORD: two young bulls, one ram, and seven male lambs a year old, ²⁸ with their grain offering of fine flour mixed with oil, six quarts with each bull, four quarts with the ram, ²⁹ and two quarts with each of the seven lambs, ³⁰ and one male goat to make atonement for yourselves. ³¹ Offer them with their drink offerings in addition to the regular burnt offering and its grain offering. Your animals are to be unblemished."

NUMBERS 29

FESTIVAL OF TRUMPETS OFFERINGS

¹ "You are to hold a sacred assembly in the seventh month, on the first day of the month, and you are not to do any daily work. This will be a day of trumpet blasts for you. ² Offer a burnt offering as a pleasing aroma to the LORD: one young bull, one ram, seven male lambs a year old—all unblemished— ³ with their grain offering of fine flour mixed with oil, six quarts with the bull, four quarts with the ram, ⁴ and two quarts with each of the seven male lambs. ⁵ Also offer one male goat as a sin offering to make atonement for yourselves. ⁶ These are in addition to the monthly and regular burnt offerings with their prescribed grain offerings and drink offerings. They are a pleasing aroma, a food offering to the LORD.

OFFERINGS FOR THE DAY OF ATONEMENT

⁷ "You are to hold a sacred assembly on the tenth day of this seventh month and practice self-denial; do not do any work. ⁸ Present a burnt offering to the LORD, a pleasing aroma: one young bull, one ram, and seven male lambs a year old. All your animals are to be unblemished. ⁹ Their grain offering is to be of fine flour mixed with oil, six quarts with the bull, four quarts with the ram, ¹⁰ and two quarts with each of the seven lambs. ¹¹ Offer one male goat for a sin offering. The regular burnt offering

with its grain offering and drink offerings are in addition to the sin offering of atonement.

OFFERINGS FOR THE FESTIVAL OF SHELTERS

[12] "You are to hold a sacred assembly on the fifteenth day of the seventh month; you do not do any daily work. You are to celebrate a seven-day festival for the LORD. [13] Present a burnt offering, a food offering, a pleasing aroma to the LORD: thirteen young bulls, two rams, and fourteen male lambs a year old. They are to be unblemished. [14] Their grain offering is to be of fine flour mixed with oil, six quarts with each of the thirteen bulls, four quarts with each of the two rams, [15] and two quarts with each of the fourteen lambs. [16] Also offer one male goat as a sin offering. These are in addition to the regular burnt offering with its grain and drink offerings.

[17] "On the second day present twelve young bulls, two rams, and fourteen male lambs a year old—all unblemished— [18] with their grain and drink offerings for the bulls, rams, and lambs, in proportion to their number. [19] Also offer one male goat as a sin offering. These are in addition to the regular burnt offering with its grain and drink and their drink offerings.

[20] "On the third day present eleven bulls, two rams, fourteen male lambs a year old—all unblemished— [21] with their grain and drink offerings for the bulls, rams, and lambs, in proportion to their number. [22] Also offer one male goat as a sin offering. These are in addition to the regular burnt offering with its grain and drink offerings.

[23] "On the fourth day present ten bulls, two rams, fourteen male lambs a year old—all unblemished— [24] with their grain and drink offerings for the bulls, rams, and lambs, in proportion to their number. [25] Also offer one male goat as a sin offering. These are in addition to the regular burnt offering with its grain and drink offerings.

[26] "On the fifth day present nine bulls, two rams, fourteen male lambs a year old—all unblemished— [27] with their grain and drink offerings for the bulls, rams, and lambs, in proportion to their number. [28] Also offer one male goat as a sin offering. These are in addition to the regular burnt offering with its grain and drink offerings.

[29] "On the sixth day present eight bulls, two rams, fourteen male lambs a year old—all unblemished— [30] with their grain and drink offerings for the bulls, rams, and lambs, in proportion to their number. [31] Also offer one male goat as a sin offering. These are in addition to the regular burnt offering with its grain and drink offerings.

[32] "On the seventh day present seven bulls, two rams, and fourteen male lambs a year old—all unblemished— [33] with their grain and drink offerings for the bulls, rams, and lambs, in proportion to their number. [34] Also offer one male goat as a sin offering. These are in addition to the regular burnt offering with its grain and drink offerings.

[35] "On the eighth day you are to hold a solemn assembly; you are not to do any daily work. [36] Present a burnt offering, a food offering, a pleasing aroma to the LORD: one bull, one ram, seven male lambs a year old—all unblemished— [37] with their grain and drink offerings for the bulls, rams, and lambs, in proportion to their number. [38] Also offer one male goat as a sin offering. These are in

addition to the regular burnt offering with its grain and drink offerings.

³⁹ "Offer these to the LORD at your appointed times in addition to your vow and freewill offerings, whether burnt, grain, drink, or fellowship offerings." ⁴⁰ So Moses told the Israelites everything the LORD had commanded him.

NUMBERS 30

REGULATIONS ABOUT VOWS

¹ Moses told the leaders of the Israelite tribes, "This is what the LORD has commanded: ² When a man makes a vow to the LORD or swears an oath to put himself under an obligation, he must not break his word; he must do whatever he has promised.

³ "When a woman in her father's house during her youth makes a vow to the LORD or puts herself under an obligation, ⁴ and her father hears about her vow or the obligation she put herself under, and he says nothing to her, all her vows and every obligation she put herself under are binding. ⁵ But if her father prohibits her on the day he hears about it, none of her vows and none of the obligations she put herself under are binding. The LORD will release her because her father has prohibited her.

⁶ "If a woman marries while her vows or the rash commitment she herself made are binding, ⁷ and her husband hears about it and says nothing to her when he finds out, her vows are binding, and the obligations she put herself under are binding. ⁸ But if her husband prohibits her when he hears about it, he will cancel her vow that is binding or the rash commitment she herself made, and the LORD will release her.

⁹ "Every vow a widow or divorced woman puts herself under is binding on her.

¹⁰ "If a woman in her husband's house has made a vow or put herself under an obligation with an oath, ¹¹ and her husband hears about it, says nothing to her, and does not prohibit her, all her vows are binding, and every obligation she put herself under is binding. ¹² But if her husband cancels them on the day he hears about it, nothing that came from her lips, whether her vows or her obligation, is binding. Her husband has canceled them, and the LORD will release her. ¹³ Her husband may confirm or cancel any vow or any sworn obligation to deny herself. ¹⁴ If her husband says nothing at all to her from day to day, he confirms all her vows and obligations, which are binding. He has confirmed them because he said nothing to her when he heard about them. ¹⁵ But if he cancels them after he hears about them, he will be responsible for her commitment."

¹⁶ These are the statutes that the LORD commanded Moses concerning the relationship between a man and his wife, or between a father and his daughter in his house during her youth.

◆ GOING DEEPER

HEBREWS 10:1-10

THE PERFECT SACRIFICE

¹ Since the law has only a shadow of the good things to come, and not the reality itself of those things, it can never perfect the worshipers by the same sacrifices they continually offer year after year. ² Otherwise, wouldn't they have stopped being offered, since the worshipers, purified once and for all, would no longer have any consciousness of sins? ³ But in the sacrifices there is a reminder of sins year after year. ⁴ For it is impossible for the blood of bulls and goats to take away sins.

⁵ Therefore, as he was coming into the world, he said:

> You did not desire sacrifice and offering,
> but you prepared a body for me.
> ⁶ You did not delight
> in whole burnt offerings and sin offerings.
> ⁷ Then I said, "See—
> it is written about me
> in the scroll—
> I have come to do your will, God."

⁸ After he says above, You did not desire or delight in sacrifices and offerings, whole burnt offerings and sin offerings (which are offered according to the law), ⁹ he then says, See, I have come to do your will. He takes away the first to establish the second. ¹⁰ By this will,

WE HAVE BEEN SANCTIFIED THROUGH THE OFFERING OF THE BODY OF JESUS CHRIST ONCE FOR ALL TIME.

NOTES

THE

DAY

TRANSJORDAN

31

SETTLEMENTS

WAR WITH MIDIAN

¹ The LORD spoke to Moses, ² "Execute vengeance for the Israelites against the Midianites. After that, you will be gathered to your people."

³ So Moses spoke to the people, "Equip some of your men for war. They will go against Midian to inflict the LORD's vengeance on them. ⁴ Send one thousand men to war from each Israelite tribe." ⁵ So one thousand were recruited from each Israelite tribe out of the thousands in Israel—twelve thousand equipped for war. ⁶ Moses sent one thousand from each tribe to war. They went with Phinehas son of Eleazar the priest, in whose care were the holy objects and signal trumpets.

⁷ They waged war against Midian, as the LORD had commanded Moses, and killed every male. ⁸ Along with the others slain by them, they killed the Midianite kings—Evi, Rekem, Zur, Hur, and Reba, the five kings of Midian. They also killed Balaam son of Beor with the sword. ⁹ The Israelites took the Midianite women and their dependents captive, and they plundered all their cattle, flocks, and property. ¹⁰ Then they burned all the cities where the Midianites lived, as well as all their encampments, ¹¹ and took away all the spoils of war and the captives, both people and animals. ¹² They brought the prisoners, animals, and spoils of war to Moses, the priest Eleazar, and the Israelite community at the camp on the plains of Moab by the Jordan across from Jericho.

¹³ Moses, the priest Eleazar, and all the leaders of the community went to meet them outside the camp. ¹⁴ But Moses became furious with the officers, the commanders of thousands and commanders of hundreds, who were returning from the military campaign. ¹⁵ "Have you let every female live?" he asked them. ¹⁶ "Yet they are the ones who, at Balaam's advice, incited the Israelites to unfaithfulness against the LORD in the Peor incident, so that the plague came against the LORD's community. ¹⁷ So now, kill every male among the dependents and kill every woman who has gone to bed with a man, ¹⁸ but keep alive for yourselves all the young females who have not gone to bed with a man.

¹⁹ "You are to remain outside the camp for seven days. All of you and your prisoners who have killed a person or touched the dead are to purify yourselves on the third day and the seventh day. ²⁰ Also purify everything: garments, leather goods, things made of goat hair, and every article of wood."

²¹ Then the priest Eleazar said to the soldiers who had gone to battle, "This is the legal statute the LORD commanded Moses: ²² The gold, silver, bronze, iron, tin, and lead— ²³ everything that can withstand fire—you are to pass through fire, and it will be clean. It must still be purified with the purification water. Anything that cannot withstand fire, pass through the water. ²⁴ On the seventh day wash your clothes, and you will be clean. After that you may enter the camp."

²⁵ The LORD told Moses, ²⁶ "You, the priest Eleazar, and the family heads of the community are to take a count of what was captured, people and animals. ²⁷ Then divide the captives between the troops who went out to war and the entire community. ²⁸ Set aside a tribute for the LORD from what belongs to the fighting men who went out to war: one out of every five

hundred people, cattle, donkeys, sheep, and goats. ²⁹ Take the tribute from their half and give it to the priest Eleazar as a contribution to the Lord. ³⁰ From the Israelites' half, take one out of every fifty from the people, cattle, donkeys, sheep, and goats, all the livestock, and give them to the Levites who perform the duties of the Lord's tabernacle."

³¹ So Moses and the priest Eleazar did as the Lord commanded Moses. ³² The captives remaining from the plunder the army had taken totaled:

675,000 sheep and goats,
³³ 72,000 cattle,
³⁴ 61,000 donkeys,
³⁵ and 32,000 people, all the females who had not gone to bed with a man.

³⁶ The half portion for those who went out to war numbered:

337,500 sheep and goats,
³⁷ and the tribute to the Lord was 675 from the sheep and goats;
³⁸ from the 36,000 cattle, the tribute to the Lord was 72;
³⁹ from the 30,500 donkeys, the tribute to the Lord was 61;
⁴⁰ and from the 16,000 people, the tribute to the Lord was 32 people.

⁴¹ Moses gave the tribute to the priest Eleazar as a contribution for the Lord, as the Lord had commanded Moses.

⁴² From the Israelites' half, which Moses separated from the men who fought, ⁴³ the community's half was:

337,500 sheep and goats,
⁴⁴ 36,000 cattle,
⁴⁵ 30,500 donkeys,
⁴⁶ and 16,000 people.

⁴⁷ Moses took one out of every fifty, selected from the people and the livestock of the Israelites' half. He gave them to the Levites who perform the duties of the Lord's tabernacle, as the Lord had commanded him.

⁴⁸ The officers who were over the thousands of the army, the commanders of thousands and of hundreds, approached Moses ⁴⁹ and told him, "Your servants have taken a census of the fighting men under our command, and not one of us is missing. ⁵⁰ So we have presented to the Lord an offering of the gold articles each man found—armlets, bracelets, rings, earrings, and necklaces—to make atonement for ourselves before the Lord."

⁵¹ Moses and the priest Eleazar received from them all the articles made out of gold. ⁵² All the

IF WE HAVE FOUND FAVOR WITH YOU, LET THIS LAND BE GIVEN TO YOUR SERVANTS AS A POSSESSION. DON'T MAKE US CROSS THE JORDAN.

NUMBERS 32:5

gold of the contribution they offered to the LORD, from the commanders of thousands and of hundreds, was 420 pounds. [53] Each of the soldiers had taken plunder for himself. [54] Moses and the priest Eleazar received the gold from the commanders of thousands and of hundreds and brought it into the tent of meeting as a memorial for the Israelites before the LORD.

NUMBERS 32

TRANSJORDAN SETTLEMENTS

[1] The Reubenites and Gadites had a very large number of livestock. When they surveyed the lands of Jazer and Gilead, they saw that the region was a good one for livestock. [2] So the Gadites and Reubenites came to Moses, the priest Eleazar, and the leaders of the community and said, [3] "The territory of Ataroth, Dibon, Jazer, Nimrah, Heshbon, Elealeh, Sebam, Nebo, and Beon, [4] which the LORD struck down before the community of Israel, is good land for livestock, and your servants own livestock." [5] They said, "If we have found favor with you, let this land be given to your servants as a possession. Don't make us cross the Jordan."

[6] But Moses asked the Gadites and Reubenites, "Should your brothers go to war while you stay here?

[7] WHY ARE YOU DISCOURAGING THE ISRAELITES FROM CROSSING INTO THE LAND THE LORD HAS GIVEN THEM?

[8] That's what your ancestors did when I sent them from Kadesh-barnea to see the land. [9] After they went up as far as Eshcol Valley and saw the land, they discouraged the Israelites from entering the land the LORD had given them. [10] So the LORD's anger burned that day, and he swore an oath: [11] 'Because they did

not remain loyal to me, none of the men twenty years old or more who came up from Egypt will see the land I swore to give Abraham, Isaac, and Jacob— ¹² none except Caleb son of Jephunneh the Kenizzite and Joshua son of Nun, because they did remain loyal to the LORD.' ¹³ The LORD's anger burned against Israel, and he made them wander in the wilderness forty years until the whole generation that had done what was evil in the LORD's sight was gone. ¹⁴ And here you, a brood of sinners, stand in your ancestors' place adding even more to the LORD's burning anger against Israel. ¹⁵ If you turn back from following him, he will once again leave this people in the wilderness, and you will destroy all of them."

¹⁶ Then they approached him and said, "We want to build sheep pens here for our livestock and cities for our dependents. ¹⁷ But we will arm ourselves and be ready to go ahead of the Israelites until we have brought them into their place. Meanwhile, our dependents will remain in the fortified cities because of the inhabitants of the land. ¹⁸ We will not return to our homes until each of the Israelites has taken possession of his inheritance. ¹⁹ Yet we will not have an inheritance with them across the Jordan and beyond, because our inheritance will be across the Jordan to the east."

²⁰ Moses replied to them, "If you do this—if you arm yourselves for battle before the LORD, ²¹ and every one of your armed men crosses the Jordan before the LORD until he has driven his enemies from his presence, ²² and the land is subdued before the LORD—afterward you may return and be free from obligation to the LORD and to Israel. And this land will belong to you as a possession before the LORD. ²³ But if you

don't do this, you will certainly sin against the LORD; be sure your sin will catch up with you. ²⁴ Build cities for your dependents and pens for your flocks, but do what you have promised."

²⁵ The Gadites and Reubenites answered Moses, "Your servants will do just as my lord commands. ²⁶ Our dependents, wives, livestock, and all our animals will remain here in the cities of Gilead, ²⁷ but your servants are equipped for war before the LORD and will go across to the battle as my lord orders."

²⁸ So Moses gave orders about them to the priest Eleazar, Joshua son of Nun, and the family heads of the Israelite tribes. ²⁹ Moses told them, "If the Gadites and Reubenites cross the Jordan with you, every man in battle formation before the LORD, and the land is subdued before you, you are to give them the land of Gilead as a possession. ³⁰ But if they don't go across with you in battle formation, they must accept land in Canaan with you."

³¹ The Gadites and Reubenites replied, "What the LORD has spoken to your servants is what we will do. ³² We will cross over in battle formation before the LORD into the land of Canaan, but we will keep our hereditary possession across the Jordan."

³³ So Moses gave them—the Gadites, Reubenites, and half the tribe of Manasseh son of Joseph—the kingdom of King Sihon of the Amorites and the kingdom of King Og of Bashan, the land including its cities with the territories surrounding them. ³⁴ The Gadites rebuilt Dibon, Ataroth, Aroer, ³⁵ Atroth-shophan, Jazer, Jogbehah, ³⁶ Beth-nimrah, and Beth-haran as fortified

cities, and built sheep pens. ³⁷ The Reubenites rebuilt Heshbon, Elealeh, Kiriathaim, ³⁸ as well as Nebo and Baal-meon (whose names were changed), and Sibmah. They gave names to the cities they rebuilt.

³⁹ The descendants of Machir son of Manasseh went to Gilead, captured it, and drove out the Amorites who were there. ⁴⁰ So Moses gave Gilead to the clan of Machir son of Manasseh, and they settled in it. ⁴¹ Jair, a descendant of Manasseh, went and captured their villages, which he renamed Jair's Villages. ⁴² Nobah went and captured Kenath with its surrounding villages and called it Nobah after his own name.

🜚 GOING DEEPER

PSALM 78:40-41, 54-55

⁴⁰ How often they rebelled against him
in the wilderness
and grieved him in the desert.
⁴¹ They constantly tested God
and provoked the Holy One of Israel.

…

⁵⁴ He brought them to his holy territory,
to the mountain his right hand acquired.
⁵⁵ He drove out nations before them.
He apportioned their inheritance by lot
and settled the tribes of Israel in their tents.

NUMBERS

The book of Numbers carefully details the Israelites' journey from Mount Sinai to the border of the promised land. Though we do not know their exact route, this map shows a general path the Israelites may have taken as they wandered through the wilderness as well as the general locations of key events in Numbers.

KEY EVENTS

(1) ISRAELITES ORGANIZE THEIR CAMP ACCORDING TO THE LORD'S INSTRUCTION

NM 2

(2) ISRAELITES COMPLAIN ABOUT FOOD AND MIRIAM AND AARON QUESTION MOSES'S LEADERSHIP

NM 11-12

(3) AFTER THE SCOUTS' REPORT, ISRAEL REFUSES TO ENTER THE PROMISED LAND

NM 13-14

(4) MOSES CANNOT ENTER THE PROMISED LAND

NM 20:1-13

(5) AARON DIES AND ELEAZAR SUCCEEDS AS PRIEST

NM 20:22-29

(6) BALAAM PRONOUNCES HIS ORACLES OVER ISRAEL

NM 23-24

(7) GOD APPOINTS JOSHUA TO SUCCEED MOSES

NM 27:12-23

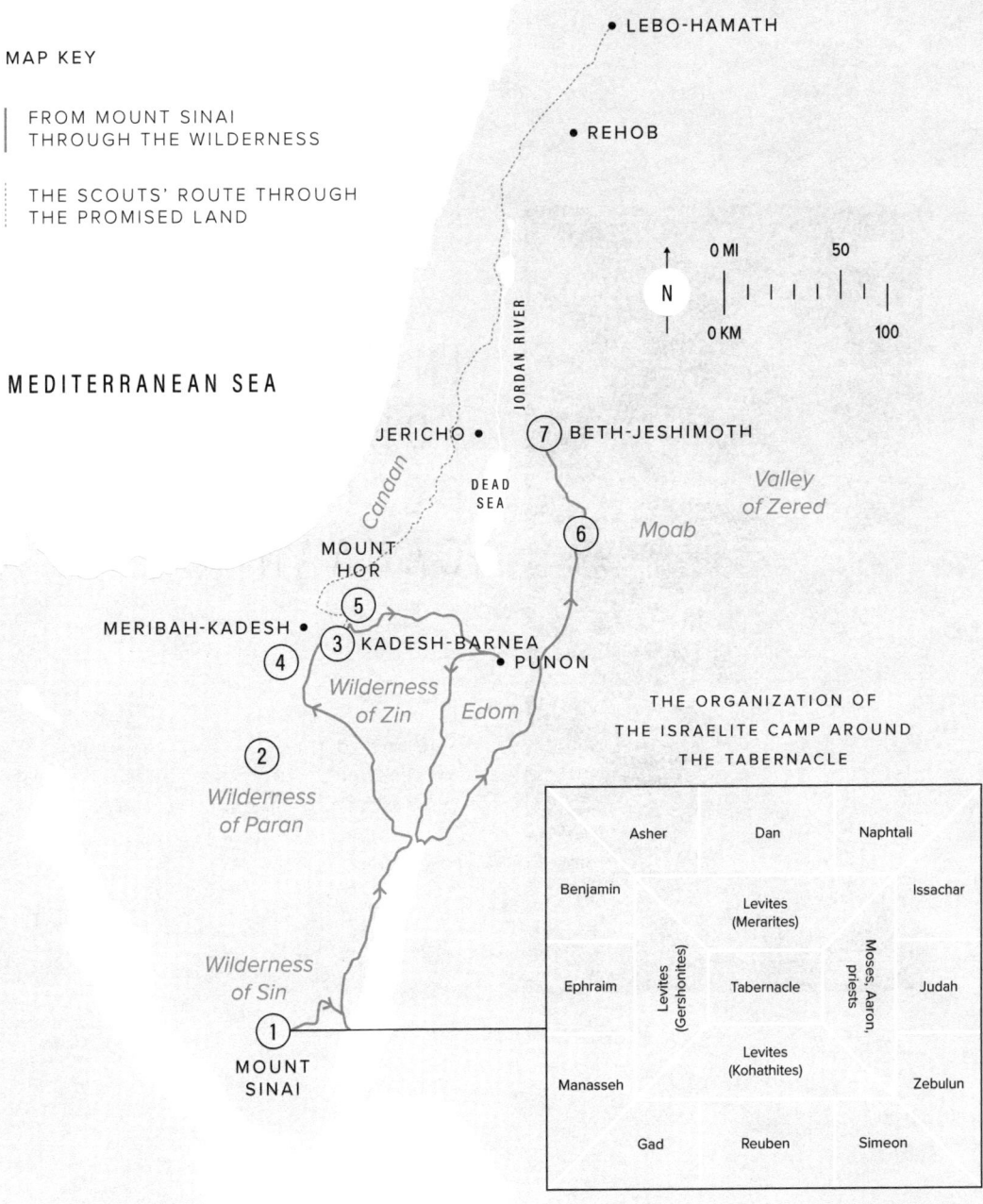

MAP KEY

| FROM MOUNT SINAI THROUGH THE WILDERNESS

⋮ THE SCOUTS' ROUTE THROUGH THE PROMISED LAND

● LEBO-HAMATH

● REHOB

N   0 MI   50

     0 KM   100

MEDITERRANEAN SEA

JORDAN RIVER

Canaan

JERICHO ●   ⑦ BETH-JESHIMOTH

DEAD SEA   *Valley of Zered*

⑥   *Moab*

MOUNT HOR

⑤

MERIBAH-KADESH ●   ③ KADESH-BARNEA

④   ● PUNON

Wilderness of Zin   *Edom*

②

THE ORGANIZATION OF
THE ISRAELITE CAMP AROUND
THE TABERNACLE

Wilderness of Paran

	Asher	Dan	Naphtali
Benjamin		Levites (Merarites)	Issachar
Ephraim	Levites (Gershonites)	Tabernacle	Moses, Aaron, priests	Judah
Manasseh		Levites (Kohathites)		Zebulun
	Gad	Reuben	Simeon

Wilderness of Sin

①

MOUNT SINAI

God manifested His presence in the
tabernacle at the center of the Israelite
camp. The cloud of God's presence guided
Israel through the wilderness, and always
settled over the tabernacle. NM 9:15–23

© 2024 He Reads Truth. All rights reserved.

INSTRUCTIONS FOR OCCUPYING CANAAN

———

"YOU ARE TO TAKE POSSESSION OF THE LAND AND SETTLE IN IT BECAUSE I HAVE GIVEN YOU THE LAND TO POSSESS."

NUMBERS 33:53

NUMBERS 33

WILDERNESS TRAVELS REVIEWED

¹ These were the stages of the Israelites' journey when they went out of the land of Egypt by their military divisions under the leadership of Moses and Aaron. ² At the LORD's command, Moses wrote down the starting points for the stages of their journey; these are the stages listed by their starting points:

³ They traveled from Rameses in the first month, on the fifteenth day of the month. On the day after the Passover the Israelites went out defiantly in the sight of all the Egyptians. ⁴ Meanwhile, the Egyptians were burying every firstborn male the LORD had struck down among them, for the LORD had executed judgment against their gods. ⁵ The Israelites traveled from Rameses and camped at Succoth.

⁶ They traveled from Succoth and camped at Etham, which is on the edge of the wilderness.

⁷ They traveled from Etham and turned back to Pi-hahiroth, which faces Baal-zephon, and they camped before Migdol.

⁸ They traveled from Pi-hahiroth and crossed through the middle of the sea into the wilderness. They took a three-day journey into the Wilderness of Etham and camped at Marah.

⁹ They traveled from Marah and came to Elim. There were twelve springs and seventy date palms at Elim, so they camped there.

¹⁰ They traveled from Elim and camped by the Red Sea.

¹¹ They traveled from the Red Sea and camped in the Wilderness of Sin.

¹² They traveled from the Wilderness of Sin and camped in Dophkah.

¹³ They traveled from Dophkah and camped at Alush.

¹⁴ They traveled from Alush and camped at Rephidim, where there was no water for the people to drink.

JESUS IN THE WILDERNESS

The Gospels of Matthew, Mark, and Luke all tell the story of Jesus being tempted in the wilderness. During their time in the wilderness, Israel demonstrated rebellion and distrust in God. However, Jesus demonstrated perfect obedience to God and trust in the Spirit during His time in the wilderness.

¹⁵ They traveled from Rephidim and camped in the Wilderness of Sinai.

¹⁶ They traveled from the Wilderness of Sinai and camped at Kibroth-hattaavah.

¹⁷ They traveled from Kibroth-hattaavah and camped at Hazeroth.

¹⁸ They traveled from Hazeroth and camped at Rithmah.

¹⁹ They traveled from Rithmah and camped at Rimmon-perez.

²⁰ They traveled from Rimmon-perez and camped at Libnah.

²¹ They traveled from Libnah and camped at Rissah.

²² They traveled from Rissah and camped at Kehelathah.

²³ They traveled from Kehelathah and camped at Mount Shepher.

²⁴ They traveled from Mount Shepher and camped at Haradah.

²⁵ They traveled from Haradah and camped at Makheloth.

²⁶ They traveled from Makheloth and camped at Tahath.

²⁷ They traveled from Tahath and camped at Terah.

²⁸ They traveled from Terah and camped at Mithkah.

²⁹ They traveled from Mithkah and camped at Hashmonah.

³⁰ They traveled from Hashmonah and camped at Moseroth.

³¹ They traveled from Moseroth and camped at Bene-jaakan.

³² They traveled from Bene-jaakan and camped at Hor-haggidgad.

³³ They traveled from Hor-haggidgad and camped at Jotbathah.

³⁴ They traveled from Jotbathah and camped at Abronah.

³⁵ They traveled from Abronah and camped at Ezion-geber.

³⁶ They traveled from Ezion-geber and camped in the Wilderness of Zin (that is, Kadesh).

³⁷ They traveled from Kadesh and camped at Mount Hor on the edge of the land of Edom. ³⁸ At the Lᴏʀᴅ's command, the priest Aaron climbed Mount Hor and died there on the first day of the fifth month in the fortieth year after the Israelites went out of the land of Egypt. ³⁹ Aaron was 123 years old when he died on Mount Hor. ⁴⁰ At that time the Canaanite king of Arad, who lived in the Negev in the land of Canaan, heard the Israelites were coming.

⁴¹ They traveled from Mount Hor and camped at Zalmonah.

⁴² They traveled from Zalmonah and camped at Punon.

⁴³ They traveled from Punon and camped at Oboth.

⁴⁴ They traveled from Oboth and camped at Iye-abarim on the border of Moab.

⁴⁵ They traveled from Iyim and camped at Dibon-gad.

⁴⁶ They traveled from Dibon-gad and camped at Almon-diblathaim.

⁴⁷ They traveled from Almon-diblathaim and camped in the Abarim range facing Nebo.

⁴⁸ They traveled from the Abarim range and camped on the plains of Moab by the Jordan across from Jericho. ⁴⁹ They camped by the Jordan from Beth-jeshimoth to the Acacia Meadow on the plains of Moab.

INSTRUCTIONS FOR OCCUPYING CANAAN

⁵⁰ The Lᴏʀᴅ spoke to Moses in the plains of Moab by the Jordan across from Jericho, ⁵¹ "Tell the Israelites: When you cross the Jordan into the land of Canaan, ⁵² you must drive out all the inhabitants of the land before you,

DESTROY ALL THEIR STONE IMAGES AND CAST IMAGES, AND DEMOLISH ALL THEIR HIGH PLACES.

NOTES

⁵³ You are to take possession of the land and settle in it because I have given you the land to possess. ⁵⁴ You are to receive the land as an inheritance by lot according to your clans. Increase the inheritance for a large clan and decrease it for a small one. Whatever place the lot indicates for someone will be his. You will receive an inheritance according to your ancestral tribes. ⁵⁵ But if you don't drive out the inhabitants of the land before you, those you allow to remain will become barbs for your eyes and thorns for your sides; they will harass you in the land where you will live. ⁵⁶ And what I had planned to do to them, I will do to you."

● GOING DEEPER

EXODUS 23:20-33

PROMISES AND WARNINGS

²⁰ "I AM GOING TO SEND AN ANGEL BEFORE YOU TO PROTECT YOU ON THE WAY AND BRING YOU TO THE PLACE I HAVE PREPARED.

²¹ Be attentive to him and listen to him. Do not defy him, because he will not forgive your acts of rebellion, for my name is in him. ²² But if you will carefully obey him and do everything I say, then I will be an enemy to your enemies and a foe to your foes. ²³ For my angel will go before you and bring you to the land of the Amorites, Hethites, Perizzites, Canaanites, Hivites, and Jebusites, and I will wipe them out. ²⁴ Do not bow in worship to their gods, and do not serve them. Do not imitate their practices. Instead, demolish them and smash their sacred pillars to pieces. ²⁵ Serve the Lord your God, and he will bless your bread and your water. I will remove illnesses from you. ²⁶ No woman will miscarry or be childless in your land. I will give you the full number of your days.

²⁷ "I will cause the people ahead of you to feel terror and will throw into confusion all the nations you come to. I will make all your enemies turn their backs to you in retreat. ²⁸ I will send hornets in front of you, and they will drive the Hivites, Canaanites, and Hethites away from you. ²⁹ I will not drive them out ahead of you in a single year; otherwise, the land would become desolate, and wild animals would multiply against you. ³⁰ I will drive them out little by little ahead of you until you have become numerous and take possession of the land. ³¹ I will set your borders from the Red Sea to the Mediterranean Sea, and from the wilderness to the Euphrates River. For I will place the inhabitants of the land under your control, and you will drive them out ahead of you. ³² You must not make a covenant with them or their gods. ³³ They must not remain in your land, or else they will make you sin against me. If you serve their gods, it will be a snare for you."

PSALM 106:34-36

³⁴ They did not destroy the peoples
as the Lord had commanded them
³⁵ but mingled with the nations
and adopted their ways.
³⁶ They served their idols,

NOTES

BOUNDARIES OF THE PROMISED LAND

NUMBERS 34

BOUNDARIES OF THE PROMISED LAND

[1] The Lord spoke to Moses, [2] "Command the Israelites and say to them: When you enter the land of Canaan, it will be allotted to you as an inheritance with these borders:

[3] Your southern side will be from the Wilderness of Zin along the boundary of Edom. Your southern border on the east will begin at the east end of the Dead Sea. [4] Your border will turn south of the Scorpions' Ascent, proceed to Zin, and end south of Kadesh-barnea. It will go to Hazar-addar and proceed to Azmon. [5] The border will turn from Azmon to the Brook of Egypt, where it will end at the Mediterranean Sea.

[6] Your western border will be the coastline of the Mediterranean Sea; this will be your western border.

[7] This will be your northern border: From the Mediterranean Sea draw a line to Mount Hor; [8] from Mount Hor draw a line to the entrance of Hamath, and the border will reach Zedad. [9] Then the border will go to Ziphron and end at Hazar-enan. This will be your northern border.

[10] For your eastern border, draw a line from Hazar-enan to Shepham. [11] The border will go down from Shepham to Riblah east of Ain. It will continue down and reach the eastern slope of the Sea of Chinnereth. [12] Then the border will go down to the Jordan and end at the Dead Sea. This will be your land defined by its borders on all sides."

[13] So Moses commanded the Israelites, "This is the land you are to receive by lot as an inheritance, which the Lord commanded

to be given to the nine and a half tribes. [14] For the tribe of Reuben's descendants and the tribe of Gad's descendants have received their inheritance according to their ancestral families, and half the tribe of Manasseh has received its inheritance. [15] The two and a half tribes have received their inheritance across the Jordan east of Jericho, toward the sunrise."

LEADERS FOR DISTRIBUTING THE LAND

[16] The LORD spoke to Moses, [17] "These are the names of the men who are to distribute the land as an inheritance for you: the priest Eleazar and Joshua son of Nun. [18] Take one leader from each tribe to distribute the land. [19] These are the names of the men:

Caleb son of Jephunneh from the tribe of Judah;
[20] Shemuel son of Ammihud from the tribe of Simeon's descendants;
[21] Elidad son of Chislon from the tribe of Benjamin;
[22] Bukki son of Jogli, a leader from the tribe of Dan's descendants;
[23] from the sons of Joseph:
Hanniel son of Ephod, a leader from the tribe of Manasseh's descendants,
[24] Kemuel son of Shiphtan, a leader from the tribe of Ephraim's descendants;
[25] Eli-zaphan son of Parnach, a leader from the tribe of Zebulun's descendants;
[26] Paltiel son of Azzan, a leader from the tribe of Issachar's descendants;
[27] Ahihud son of Shelomi, a leader from the tribe of Asher's descendants;
[28] Pedahel son of Ammihud, a leader from the tribe of Naphtali's descendants."

[29] These are the ones the LORD commanded to distribute the inheritance to the Israelites in the land of Canaan.

CITIES OF REFUGE

Cities of refuge served as asylums for those who had committed involuntary manslaughter. This prevented God's people from endlessly feuding and taking revenge on one another for deaths in their families. The author of Hebrews wrote about how the hope of Christ is our own place of refuge (Heb 6:18). Under the new covenant, Christ's blood justifies us and provides a refuge to us from the wrath of death (Rm 5:9).

NUMBERS 35

CITIES FOR THE LEVITES

¹ The LORD again spoke to Moses in the plains of Moab by the Jordan across from Jericho: ² "Command the Israelites to give cities out of their hereditary property for the Levites to live in and pastureland around the cities. ³ The cities will be for them to live in, and their pasturelands will be for their herds, flocks, and all their other animals. ⁴ The pasturelands of the cities you are to give the Levites will extend from the city wall five hundred yards on every side. ⁵ Measure a thousand yards outside the city for the east side, a thousand yards for the south side, a thousand yards for the west side, and a thousand yards for the north side, with the city in the center. This will belong to them as pasturelands for the cities.

⁶ "The cities you give the Levites will include six cities of refuge, which you will provide so that the one who kills someone may flee there; in addition to these, give forty-two other cities. ⁷ The total number of cities you give the Levites will be forty-eight, along with their pasturelands. ⁸ Of the cities that you give from the Israelites' territory, you should take more from a larger tribe and less from a smaller one. Each tribe is to give some of its cities to the Levites in proportion to the inheritance it receives."

CITIES OF REFUGE

⁹ The LORD said to Moses, ¹⁰ "Speak to the Israelites and tell them: When you cross the Jordan into the land of Canaan, ¹¹ designate cities to serve as cities of refuge for you, so that a person who kills someone unintentionally may flee there. ¹² You will have the cities as a refuge from the avenger, so that the one who kills someone will not die until he stands trial before the assembly. ¹³ The cities you select will be your six cities of refuge. ¹⁴ Select three cities across the Jordan and three cities in the land of Canaan to be cities of refuge. ¹⁵ These six cities will serve as a

refuge for the Israelites and for the alien or temporary resident among them, so that anyone who kills a person unintentionally may flee there.

16 "If anyone strikes a person with an iron object and death results, he is a murderer; the murderer must be put to death. 17 If anyone has in his hand a stone capable of causing death and strikes another person and he dies, the murderer must be put to death. 18 If anyone has in his hand a wooden object capable of causing death and strikes another person and he dies, the murderer must be put to death. 19 The avenger of blood himself is to kill the murderer; when he finds him, he is to kill him. 20 Likewise, if anyone in hatred pushes a person or throws an object at him with malicious intent and he dies, 21 or if in hostility he strikes him with his hand and he dies, the one who struck him must be put to death; he is a murderer. The avenger of blood is to kill the murderer when he finds him.

22 "But if anyone suddenly pushes a person without hostility or throws any object at him without malicious intent 23 or without looking drops a stone that could kill a person and he dies, but he was not his enemy and didn't intend to harm him, 24 the assembly is to judge between the person who kills someone and the avenger of blood according to these ordinances. 25 The assembly is to protect the one who kills someone from the avenger of blood. Then the assembly will return him to the city of refuge he fled to, and he must live there until the death of the high priest who was anointed with the holy oil.

26 "If the one who kills someone ever goes outside the border of the city of refuge he fled to, 27 and the avenger of blood finds him outside the border of his city of refuge and kills him, the avenger will not be guilty of bloodshed, 28 for the one who killed a person was supposed to live in his city of refuge until the death of the high priest. Only after the death of the high priest may the one who has killed a

person return to the land he possesses. ²⁹ These instructions will be a statutory ordinance for you throughout your generations wherever you live.

³⁰ "If anyone kills a person, the murderer is to be put to death based on the word of witnesses. But no one is to be put to death based on the testimony of one witness. ³¹ You are not to accept a ransom for the life of someone who is guilty of murder; he must be put to death. ³² Neither should you accept a ransom for the person who flees to his city of refuge, allowing him to return and live in the land before the death of the high priest.

³³ "Do not defile the land where you live, for bloodshed defiles the land, and there can be no atonement for the land because of the blood that is shed on it, except by the blood of the person who shed it. ³⁴ Do not make the land unclean where you live and where I dwell; for I, the LORD, reside among the Israelites."

NUMBERS 36

THE INHERITANCE OF ZELOPHEHAD'S DAUGHTERS

¹ The family heads from the clan of the descendants of Gilead—the son of Machir, son of Manasseh—who were from the clans of the sons of Joseph, approached and addressed Moses and the leaders who were heads of the Israelite families. ² They said, "The LORD commanded my lord to give the land as an inheritance by lot to the Israelites. My lord was further commanded by the LORD to give our brother Zelophehad's inheritance to his daughters. ³ If they marry any of the men from the other Israelite tribes, their inheritance will be taken away from our fathers' inheritance and added to that of the tribe into which they marry. Therefore, part of our allotted inheritance would be taken away. ⁴ When the Jubilee comes for the Israelites, their inheritance will be added to that of the tribe into which they marry, and their inheritance will be taken away from the inheritance of our ancestral tribe."

⁵ So Moses commanded the Israelites at the word of the LORD, "What the tribe of Joseph's descendants says is right. ⁶ This is what the LORD has commanded concerning Zelophehad's daughters: They may marry anyone they like provided they marry within a clan of their ancestral tribe. ⁷ No inheritance belonging to the Israelites is to transfer from tribe to tribe, because each of the Israelites is to retain the inheritance of his ancestral tribe. ⁸ Any daughter who possesses an inheritance from an Israelite tribe must marry someone from the clan of her ancestral tribe, so that each of the Israelites will possess the inheritance of his fathers. ⁹ No inheritance is to transfer from one tribe to another, because each of the Israelite tribes is to retain its inheritance."

¹⁰ The daughters of Zelophehad did as the LORD commanded Moses. ¹¹ Mahlah, Tirzah, Hoglah, Milcah, and Noah, the daughters of Zelophehad, married cousins on their father's side. ¹² They married men from the clans of the descendants of Manasseh son of Joseph, and their inheritance remained within the tribe of their father's clan.

¹³ These are the commands and ordinances the LORD commanded the Israelites through Moses in the plains of Moab by the Jordan across from Jericho.

PSALM 16:6

The boundary lines have fallen for me
in pleasant places;
indeed, I have a beautiful inheritance.

HEBREWS 4:1-7

THE PROMISED REST

[1] Therefore, since the promise to enter his rest remains, let us beware that none of you be found to have fallen short. [2] For we also have received the good news just as they did. But the message they heard did not benefit them, since they were not united with those who heard it in faith. [3] For we who have believed enter the rest, in keeping with what he has said,

So I swore in my anger,
"They will not enter my rest,"

even though his works have been finished since the foundation of the world. [4] For somewhere he has spoken about the seventh day in this way: And on the seventh day God rested from all his works. [5] Again, in that passage he says, They will never enter my rest. [6] Therefore, since it remains for some to enter it, and those who formerly received the good news did not enter because of disobedience, [7] he again specifies a certain day—today. He specified this speaking through David after such a long time:

Today, if you hear his voice,
do not harden your hearts.

WEEK 05 RESPONSE

OBSERVE

IN THIS WEEK'S READING, HOW DID YOU OBSERVE
GOD LEADING OR RESPONDING TO HIS PEOPLE?

HOW DID GOD'S PEOPLE RESPOND TO GOD OR HIS INSTRUCTION?

WHAT QUESTIONS DO YOU HAVE?

REFLECT

Where have you seen God's love, faithfulness, forgiveness, and/or justice around you this week?

LOVE	FAITHFULNESS

FORGIVENESS	JUSTICE

NUMBERS 14:18

THE LORD IS SLOW TO ANGER AND ABOUNDING IN FAITHFUL LOVE, FORGIVING INIQUITY AND REBELLION. BUT HE WILL NOT LEAVE THE GUILTY UNPUNISHED, BRINGING THE CONSEQUENCES OF THE FATHERS' INIQUITY ON THE CHILDREN TO THE THIRD AND FOURTH GENERATION.

© 2024 He Reads Truth. All rights reserved.

GRACE

Take this day to catch up on your reading,
pray, and rest in the presence of the Lord.

———

"I AM GOING TO SEND AN ANGEL
BEFORE YOU TO PROTECT YOU ON
THE WAY AND BRING YOU TO THE
PLACE I HAVE PREPARED."

EXODUS 23:20

DAY

WEEK

05

WEEKLY

Scripture is God-breathed and true. When we memorize it,
we carry His Word with us wherever we go.

During this reading plan, we have been memorizing
Numbers 14:18. Spend some time putting it all together
as you reflect on the reality of God's character.

———

See tips for memorizing Scripture on page 180.

TRUTH

THE LORD IS SLOW TO ANGER AND ABOUNDING
IN FAITHFUL LOVE, FORGIVING INIQUITY AND
REBELLION. BUT HE WILL NOT LEAVE THE GUILTY
UNPUNISHED, BRINGING THE CONSEQUENCES OF
THE FATHERS' INIQUITY ON THE CHILDREN TO
THE THIRD AND FOURTH GENERATION.

NUMBERS 14:18

BENEDICTION

"MAY THE LORD BLESS YOU AND PROTECT YOU;
MAY THE LORD MAKE HIS FACE SHINE ON YOU
AND BE GRACIOUS TO YOU; MAY THE LORD LOOK
WITH FAVOR ON YOU AND GIVE YOU PEACE."

NUMBERS 6:24-26

Tips for Memorizing Scripture

At He Reads Truth, we believe Scripture memorization is an important discipline in your walk with God. Committing God's Truth to memory means He can minister to us—and we can minister to others—through His Word no matter where we are. As you approach the Weekly Truth passage in this book, try these memorization tips to see which techniques work best for you.

STUDY IT

Study the passage in its biblical context and ask yourself a few questions before you begin to memorize it: What does this passage say? What does it mean? How would I say this in my own words? What does it teach me about God? Understanding what the passage means helps you know why it is important to carry it with you wherever you go.

Break the passage into smaller sections, memorizing a phrase at a time.

PRAY IT

Use the passage you are memorizing as a prompt for prayer.

WRITE IT

Dedicate a notebook to Scripture memorization and write the passage over and over again.

Diagram the passage after you write it out. Place a square around the verbs, underline the nouns, and circle any adjectives or adverbs. Say the passage aloud several times, emphasizing the verbs as you repeat it. Then do the same thing again with the nouns, then the adjectives and adverbs.

Write out the first letter of each word in the passage somewhere you can reference it throughout the week as you work on your memorization.

Use a whiteboard to write out the passage. Erase a few words at a time as you continue to repeat it aloud. Keep erasing parts of the passage until you have it all committed to memory.

© 2021 He Reads Truth. All rights reserved.

CREATE

If you can, make up a tune for the passage to sing as you go about your day, or try singing it to the tune of a favorite song.

Use hand signals or signs to come up with associations for each word or phrase and repeat the movements as you practice.

SAY IT

Repeat the passage out loud to yourself as you are going through the rhythm of your day—getting ready, pouring your coffee, waiting in traffic, or making dinner.

Listen to the passage read aloud to you.

Record a voice memo on your phone and listen to it throughout the day or play it on an audio Bible.

SHARE IT

Memorize the passage with a friend, family member, or mentor. Spontaneously challenge each other to recite the passage, or pick a time to review your passage and practice saying it from memory together.

Send the passage as an encouraging text to a friend, testing yourself as you type to see how much you have memorized so far.

KEEP AT IT

Set reminders on your phone to prompt you to practice your passage.

Keep a stack of note cards with Scripture you are memorizing by your bed. Practice reciting what you've memorized previously before you go to sleep, ending with the passages you are currently learning. If you wake up in the middle of the night, review them again instead of grabbing your phone. Read them out loud before you get out of bed in the morning.

CSB BOOK ABBREVIATIONS

OLD TESTAMENT

GN Genesis	**JB** Job	**HAB** Habakkuk	**PHP** Philippians
EX Exodus	**PS** Psalms	**ZPH** Zephaniah	**COL** Colossians
LV Leviticus	**PR** Proverbs	**HG** Haggai	**1TH** 1 Thessalonians
NM Numbers	**EC** Ecclesiastes	**ZCH** Zechariah	**2TH** 2 Thessalonians
DT Deuteronomy	**SG** Song of Solomon	**MAL** Malachi	**1TM** 1 Timothy
JOS Joshua	**IS** Isaiah		**2TM** 2 Timothy
JDG Judges	**JR** Jeremiah	**NEW TESTAMENT**	**TI** Titus
RU Ruth	**LM** Lamentations		**PHM** Philemon
1SM 1 Samuel	**EZK** Ezekiel	**MT** Matthew	**HEB** Hebrews
2SM 2 Samuel	**DN** Daniel	**MK** Mark	**JMS** James
1KG 1 Kings	**HS** Hosea	**LK** Luke	**1PT** 1 Peter
2KG 2 Kings	**JL** Joel	**JN** John	**2PT** 2 Peter
1CH 1 Chronicles	**AM** Amos	**AC** Acts	**1JN** 1 John
2CH 2 Chronicles	**OB** Obadiah	**RM** Romans	**2JN** 2 John
EZR Ezra	**JNH** Jonah	**1CO** 1 Corinthians	**3JN** 3 John
NEH Nehemiah	**MC** Micah	**2CO** 2 Corinthians	**JD** Jude
EST Esther	**NAH** Nahum	**GL** Galatians	**RV** Revelation
		EPH Ephesians	

BIBLIOGRAPHY

Adair, James R., Jr. "Oracle." In *Eerdmans Dictionary of the Bible,* edited by David N. Freedman, Allen C. Myers, and Astrid B. Beck. Grand Rapids: W.B. Eerdmans, 2000.

Cole, R. Dennis. *Numbers.* Vol. 3B. The New American Commentary. Nashville: Broadman & Holman Publishers, 2000.

DeClaissé-Walford, S. G. "Refuge, Cities of." In *The International Standard Bible Encyclopedia*, edited by Geoffrey W. Bromiley et al. rev. ed. Grand Rapids: Wm. B. Eerdmans, 1979–1988.

Drouhard, R.L. "Edom." In *The Lexham Bible Dictionary,* edited by John D. Barry et al. Bellingham: Lexham Press, 2016.

Fleenor, Rob. "Midianites" In *The Lexham Bible Dictionary,* edited by John D. Barry et al. Bellingham: Lexham Press, 2016.

Hill, Andrew E. "The Spatial Syntax of Israel's Tabernacle (Exod 25:1–31:11; 35:1–40:38; Num 2:1–34; 10:11–28)," in *Lexham Geographic Commentary on the Pentateuch,* edited by Barry J. Beitzel, Lexham Geographic Commentary. Bellingham: Lexham Press, 2022.

House, Paul R. *Old Testament Theology.* Downers Grove: InterVarsity Press, 1998.

Naylor, Peter John. "Numbers." In *New Bible Commentary,* edited by D. A. Carson et al. 4th ed. Downers Grove: InterVarsity Press, 1994.

Porter, H. "Amalek, Amalekite." In *The International Standard Bible Encyclopedia,* edited by Geoffrey W. Bromiley et al. rev. ed. Grand Rapids: Wm. B. Eerdmans, 1979–1988.

Raccah, William. "Sociology and the Old Testament." In *The Lexham Bible Dictionary,* edited by John D. Barry et al. Bellingham: Lexham Press, 2016.

Springer, J. Arthur. "Cloud." In *The Wycliffe Bible Encyclopedia,* edited by Charles F. Pfeiffer, Howard F. Vos, and John Rea. Chicago: Moody Press, 1975.

Wenham, Gordon J. *Numbers: An Introduction & Commentary.* Tyndale Old Testament Commentaries. Downers Grove: InterVarsity Press, 1981.

Nelson's New Illustrated Bible Dictionary, edited by Ronald F. Youngblood. Nashville: Thomas Nelson, 1995.

YOUR DAILY GUIDE TO READING GOD'S WORD

AUTOMATICALLY DELIVERED TO YOU EACH AND EVERY MONTH

If you are looking to establish a habit of daily Bible reading or to grow in your knowledge and understanding of Scripture, look no further. Sign up today and receive our latest Daily Reading Guide delivered to your doorstep monthly.

NEVER AGAIN

WILL YOU QUESTION

Where to Start

What to Read Today

What to Read Tomorrow

GET ALL OF THIS FOR 23% OFF THE COVER PRICE OF A SINGLE DAILY READING GUIDE.

SURE, YOU CAN PURCHASE EACH PLAN SEPARATELY. HOWEVER, WITH OUR SUBSCRIPTION, YOU'LL RECEIVE

1

Consistent Delivery of Trusted Content

2

Automatic Delivery of Each Book

3

Reading Materials Each Month

4

23% Savings on Every Book

And a variety of biblical content throughout the year that includes both topical reading and reading through the books of the Bible.

 HE READS TRUTH

LEARN MORE AND SUBSCRIBE AT
SHOPSHEREADSTRUTH.COM/HRTNUMBERS

You just spent 35 days in the Word of God.

My favorite day of this reading plan:

How did I find delight in God's Word?

One thing I learned about God:

What was God doing in my life during this study?

What did I learn that I want to share with someone else?

A specific passage or verse that encouraged me:

A specific passage or verse that challenged and convicted me: